GCSE Spanish by RSL

Volume 1: Listening, Speaking

Visit **www.rsleducational.co.uk/spanishaudio** to download:

➤ Audio material for use with the listening papers in this pack.

➤ Example oral exam conversations.

This pack contains:

➤ **Four listening papers with detailed solutions**.

➤ An **oral (speaking) primer** with advice, marking guidance and analysis of the downloadable sample conversations.

➤ *Steps to a Higher Grade*: How to boost your written and oral responses.

The listening papers are modelled on papers set by all exam boards for their 9-1 GCSE syllabuses, and cover an extensive range of topics. The questions become progressively more challenging in each paper, from 'warm-up' questions to more advanced comprehension exercises.

The papers are accompanied by highly detailed, *teaching* solution pages and mark schemes. These will guide you through the questions, step-by-step – like having a personal tutor alongside you.

When used together with *Volume 2: Reading, Writing, Translation*, this pack offers thorough preparation for an excellent performance at GCSE.

How to use this pack

When correcting your work, it's a good idea to take notes of any important learning points, as well as your mistakes: this will make your revision easier. If an answer can be improved, it's worthwhile to repeat it, referring to the examples. Where alternative methods and solutions are suggested, it's often useful to try them out – to find out whether they work for you.

You can attempt these papers with or without time limits. Either way, I recommend working though the solution pages carefully, until you fully understand all the advice.

A note on exam boards

These papers are relevant to **all exam boards**. Cambridge IGCSE and Edexcel (GCSE and IGCSE) exams require some answers to be written in Spanish. Therefore, some of the questions in each listening paper ask you to answer in Spanish. Other boards tend to require answers in English.

I hope you enjoy working through this pack.

We are a family business in a competitive marketplace. We are constantly improving and expanding our range, in order to publish ever-better resources for our customers – in particular, families who find that our books offer better value than expensive private tuition.

If you have any feedback or questions, please let us know! You can get in touch through our website at **www.rsleducational.co.uk**, where you can also view our up-to-date range of publications, or by emailing **robert@rsleducational.co.uk**.

If you like this product, please tell your friends and write a review on Amazon!

Also available

➢ GCSE Spanish by RSL, Volume 2: Reading, Writing, Translation
➢ GCSE Maths by RSL (Non-Calculator: Higher Level)
➢ GCSE French by RSL
➢ GCSE German by RSL
➢ RSL 11+ Comprehension: Volumes 1 and 2
➢ RSL 11+ Maths
➢ RSL 8+ to 10+ Comprehension
➢ RSL 13+ Comprehension
➢ *11 Plus Lifeline* (printable Comprehension, Maths, Creative Writing and Reasoning resources): **www.11pluslifeline.com**

GCSE Spanish by RSL, Volume 1: Listening, Speaking
By Matt Lim
Published by RSL Educational
Copyright © RSL Educational Ltd 2018

Table of Contents

Topic Guide

The same core topics are tested by all exam boards, sometimes with slightly different titles (and often with a fair bit of crossover between the sub-topics listed below, depending on the board).

Home and Abroad

- ✓ Town and rural life
- ✓ Weather and climate
- ✓ Everyday life and traditions abroad
- ✓ Holidays and tourism
- ✓ Services such as using the phone, bank, post office
- ✓ Travel, transport and directions

Education and Employment

- ✓ School life
- ✓ School routine
- ✓ Childhood
- ✓ Future plans
- ✓ Jobs and careers

House, Home and Daily Routine

- ✓ Types of home
- ✓ Self, family, friends and relationships
- ✓ Household chores
- ✓ Food and drink

The Modern World and the Environment

- ✓ Technology and information e.g. Internet, mobile phones, social media
- ✓ Environmental issues
- ✓ Current affairs and social issues
- ✓ The media e.g. TV, film, newspapers

Social Activities, Fitness and Health

- ✓ Hobbies, pastimes, sports and exercise
- ✓ Shopping and money
- ✓ Celebrations
- ✓ Accidents, injuries and health issues

Listening Paper 1

*Visit **www.rsleducational.co.uk/spanishaudio** to download the audio file for this paper.*

If you wish to complete this paper in timed conditions, allow 45 minutes plus 5 minutes' reading time.

Instructions

- Use **black** ink or ballpoint pen.
- Answer **all** questions.
- Answer the questions in the spaces provided.
  - *There may be more space than you require.*
- Dictionaries are **not** allowed.

Advice

- You have 5 minutes to read through the paper before the recording starts.
- You will hear each extract twice. You may write at any time during the examination. There will be a pause between each question.
- Read each question **carefully** before attempting it.
- The marks available for each question are given in [square brackets]. These give you an indication of how long to spend on each question.
- There is a total of **50 marks** available for this paper.
- Leave time to check your answers at the end, if possible.

Answer ALL questions.

En el restaurante

1   ¿Qué **cuatro** alimentos se mencionan? Pon una equis **[X]** en cada casilla correcta.

Which **four** foods are mentioned? Put a cross **[X]** in each correct box.

(Total for Question 1 = 4 marks)

El fin de semana

2   ¿Adónde van estas personas?

Where are these people going?

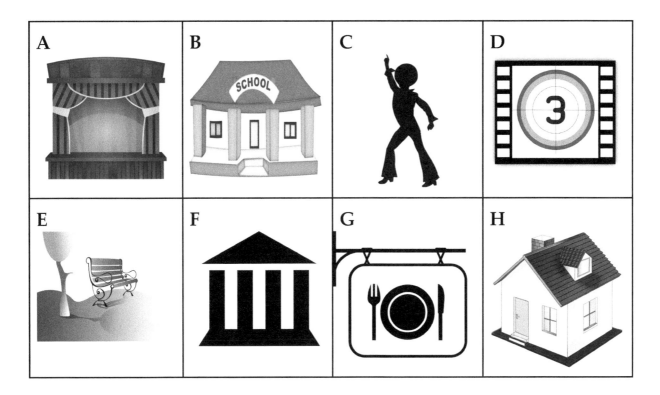

Escribe la letra correcta en cada casilla.
Write the correct letter in each box.

Ejemplo	E
(a)	
(b)	
(c)	

(Total for Question 2 = 3 marks)

Mi vida personal

3   Rocío está hablando sobre su vida. ¿Qué menciona? Pon una equis **[X]** en cada casilla correcta.

Rocío is talking about her life. What does she mention? Put a cross **[X]** in each correct box.

Ejemplo: Rocío es de…

(a) Su deporte favorito es el…

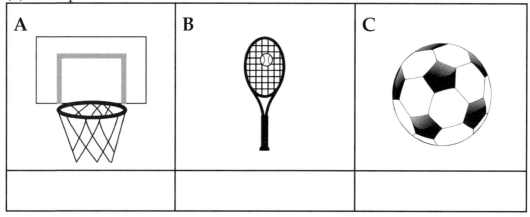

(b) A Rocío también le gusta…

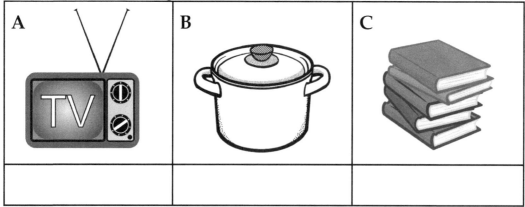

(c) Los fines de semana…

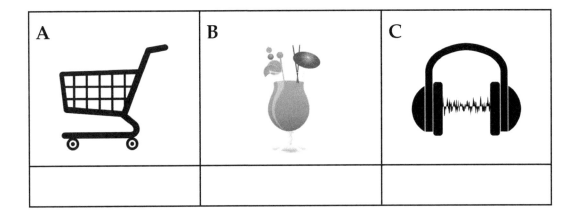

(d) Trabaja en…

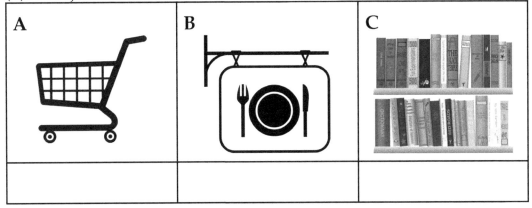

(e) Va a ir de vacaciones a…

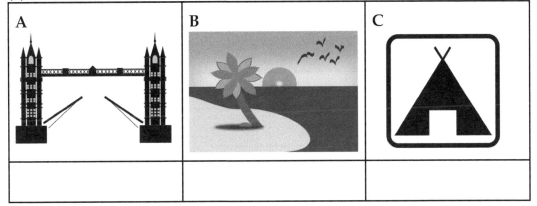

(Total for Question 3 = 5 marks)

Tareas domésticas

4   ¿Cómo ayudan estos jóvenes en casa? Pon una equis **[X]** en cada casilla correcta.

How do these young people help at home? Put a cross **[X]** in each correct box.

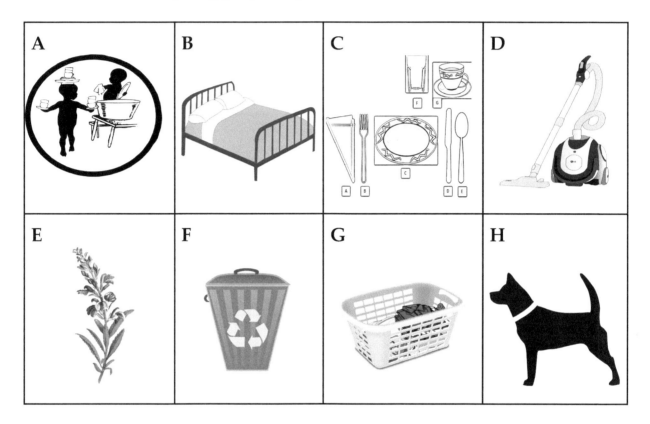

	A	B	C	D	E	F	G	H
Ejemplo: Cai								X
(a) Jorge								
(b) Luisa								
(c) Sonia								
(d) Carlitos								
(e) Micaela								

(Total for Question 4 = 5 marks)

Mi colegio

5　　María Josefa habla de su asignatura favorita. ¿Qué dice? Completa las frases con las letras correctas.

María Josefa is talking about her favourite subject. What does she say? Complete the phrases with the correct letters.

A Jueves	**B** Ciencias	**C** Estricta
D Médica	**E** Simpática	**F** Lunes
G Gorda	**H** Profesora	**I** Matemáticas

Ejemplo: Su asignatura favorita son las ...	I
(a) Su día escolar favorito es el ...	
(b) La profesora es ...	
(c) Quiere trabajar como ...	

(Total for Question 5 = 3 marks)

El libro azul de Colombia

6 Escucha este informe sobre Colombia y contesta la pregunta que está debajo.

Listen to this report about Colombia and answer the question below.

¿Qué **seis** frases son correctas? Pon una equis **[X]** en cada casilla apropiada.
Which **six** statements are correct? Put a cross **[X]** in each correct box.

Ejemplo: El "Libro azul" tiene una cubierta de color azul y oro.	X
(a) El libro está lleno de imágenes.	
(b) El libro es monocromático.	
(c) Fue encargado por el actual presidente de Colombia.	
(d) Fue diseñado para promover Colombia en otros países mundiales.	
(e) Está escrito en inglés y español.	
(f) La historia política de Colombia es muy turbulenta.	
(g) Hoy en día, Colombia es un símbolo de modernización.	
(h) El libro hace mucha referencia al estado económico del país.	
(i) Contiene música escrita por un conductor colombiano famoso.	
(j) Se celebran las habilidades y logros de las mujeres colombianas.	
(k) Muchos expertos quieren comprarlo pero es casi imposible.	
(l) Sin embargo, el libro está disponible en línea.	

(Total for Question 6 = 6 marks)

Entrevista con una actriz

7   Escucha esta entrevista con una actriz sobre sus experiencias. Después, contesta las preguntas que están debajo **en inglés**.

Listen to this interview with an actress about her experiences. Then answer the questions below **in English**.

(a) How does she describe the director?   [1]

....

(b) (i) Give **two** things that she admires about the director.   [2]

....

....

(ii) Why does she compare him to a spider?   [1]

....

(c) What was her reaction to the film they worked on? Give **two** ideas.   [2]

....

....

(d) What is the message of the film, according to her?   [1]

....

(e) What **personal** reason does she give for why this film is so special to her?

[1]

....

(Total for Question 7 = 8 marks)

¿Universidad o no?

8   Estas personas están discutiendo la importancia de ir a la universidad. Escribe **en español** en la tabla las razones por las que se debe ir a la universidad, y aquellas por las que no se debe ir. No tienes que escribir en frases completas, pero debes usar cada casilla disponible.

These people are discussing the importance of going to university. Write **in Spanish** in the grid below the reasons why one should go to university and the reasons why one shouldn't. You don't have to write in full sentences but you should use every available box.

Razones para ir a la universidad
Ejemplo: Conocer a gente nueva

Razones para no ir a la universidad

(**Total for Question 8 = 6 marks**)

Regreso de Argentina

9   Tu amiga ha vuelto de Argentina. Escucha la grabación y contesta las preguntas **en español.**

Your friend has returned from Argentina. Listen to the recording and answer the questions **in Spanish.**

(a) (i) ¿Cuánto tiempo llevaba en Argentina?   [1]

……………………………………………………………………………………………

(ii) ¿Por qué ha vuelto ahora?   [1]

……………………………………………………………………………………………

(b) (i) A tu amiga, ¿qué aspectos de Argentina le gustan? Da **dos** ideas.   [2]

……………………………………………………………………………………………

……………………………………………………………………………………………

(ii) ¿Qué es lo que **no** le gusta?   [1]

……………………………………………………………………………………………

(c) Da **dos** consejos para ir a Argentina.   [2]

……………………………………………………………………………………………

……………………………………………………………………………………………

(d) ¿Qué perdió su amiga en Buenos Aires?   [1]

……………………………………………………………………………………………

(e) ¿Le gustaría volver a Argentina en el futuro? ¿Por qué/por qué no?   [2]

....

....

(Total for Question 9 = 10 marks)

TOTAL FOR PAPER = 50 MARKS

Blank Page

Listening Paper 1 – SOLUTIONS

En el restaurante

---

1 ¿Qué cuatro alimentos se mencionan?

    (a) (d) (g) (i)   [4]

This is a simple question to get you used to the speed and style of the recording. It tests some fairly simple core GCSE vocabulary. Normally the title at the top of each section will give you a clue as to what area of vocabulary is being tested: in this case, restaurants and food.

You are required to put a cross underneath the pictures once you hear the Spanish word(s) in the dialogue. There are **four** marks available for this question. Therefore, you need to cross exactly four boxes! If you check the wrong number, you will lose marks.

In this piece, the answers do not necessarily occur in the dialogue in the same order as the pictures. However, three of the items are mentioned more than once.

TOP TIP: Bring a pencil (and an eraser)!

The **first time** you hear the recording, make notes in pencil. You can also put a cross next to the answers you think are right (i.e. **not** in the answer box itself). Make sure to keep listening while you are doing this!

You can also **cross out** each picture in pencil once you have used it, so you can see quickly and clearly which ones are left. Do this neatly, however, in case you make a mistake and need to repeat the question.

The recording will then play a **second time**, giving you chance to check and confirm your answers. There will be a short pause after the first recording, and after the second time you hear it. Use this time to go over the crosses you are confident about with a black pen, and erase any that are incorrect.

Below is a transcript, with the key information given **in bold**.

Full Transcript
M: *Buenos días señora. ¿Ha decidido qué quiere?*
F: *Hola, no estoy segura. ¿Hay algo con **patatas fritas**?*
M: *Sí, claro. Todas **las hamburguesas** vienen con **patatas fritas**.*

F: *Pero no tengo mucha hambre.*

M: *Puede tomar **una ensalada** en vez de **patatas fritas**.*

F: *Es que **una hamburguesa** tiene demasiada grasa. Me quedo con **el pollo** y una **ensalada** pequeña.*

M: *Vale, señora.*

Mark Scheme:

0-4	- Award one mark for each correct answer, up to four. - Deduct one mark for each incorrect answer, even if the correct answers are also crossed. - *Therefore, crossing eight boxes would mean four wrong answers, scoring 0 marks.*

El fin de semana

2 ¿Adónde van estas personas?	
(a) B	[1]
(b) H	[1]
(c) F	[1]

There are three marks available for this question: one per correct answer. You will hear each person twice, including the example.

TOP TIP: Pay attention to the whole sentence.

If you don't know the meaning of the key word in the recording, or if you forget it, keep listening to the rest of the sentence for clues. For example, in **2(a)** he has to go to *cole*; if you didn't know that this was short for *colegio*, he also says the reason they have to go is because there is *un examen de biología*.

A common mistake is to stop listening once you think you have heard the right answer: you need to pay attention to the entire sentence in case there are traps. For example, in **2(b)** Marta is **unable** to go to the cinema because she is ill, so decides to stay at home instead. However, some more trigger-happy students will not have noticed that bit, as they will just have heard *cine* and rushed to tick the incorrect box.

Similarly, in **2(c)**, the important information is the science <u>museum</u>. The mention of science *classes* is a trap (bear in mind that "school" has already occurred as an answer).

Full Transcript

Ejemplo: M: *Esta tarde vamos al **parque** a jugar al fútbol y tomar el sol.*

(a) M: *Tenemos que ir al **cole** porque hay un exámen de biología por la tarde y hay que aprobar.*

(b) F: *¡Hola! Soy Marta. Lo siento, pero no puedo ir al cine esta noche porque estoy enferma. Voy a quedarme **en casa**.*

(c) F: *Voy a visitar el **museo de ciencia** porque me fascinan mis clases de química.*

Mark Scheme:

0-3	- Award one mark for each correct answer, up to three. - Incorrect answers do not score. Multiple answers score 0 marks for that question.

Mi vida personal

3 ¿Rocío está hablando sobre su vida. ¿Qué menciona?	
(a) A	[1]
(b) C	[1]
(c) A	[1]
(d) B	[1]
(e) B	[1]

There are pauses in this recording, which allow you to make notes and choose your answers. Listen out for clues and for traps. The exact words for each answer may not be used in the recording, so look out for synonyms and key phrases, then use common sense and a process of elimination to arrive at the correct answer.

3(a) Rocío mentions that she plays a lot of tennis but then uses *sin embargo* to introduce a second sport that she prefers (*que más me gusta*): basketball.

3(b) She then talks about what she does to relax when she is not being active: reading books or magazines.

3(c) She mentions that she goes shopping on Saturdays and spends a lot of money on clothes. Either of those things would point to option **A**.

3(d) She works as a waitress during the week (option **B**), which she hates because of the food and the customers. Again, any of this information would give you the correct answer.

3(e) Finally, she simply says she is going to the beach next week.

Full Transcript - Answers are given in **bold,** clues are <u>underlined</u>, and traps are both <u>**underlined and bold**</u>.

Ejemplo: F: *Hola, me llamo Rocío. Soy una chica **española** normal.*

(a) *Me gusta ser muy activa y **<u>juego al tenis</u>** dos veces a la semana. <u>Sin embargo</u>, el deporte que <u>más me gusta</u> es el **baloncesto** porque es muy emocionante.*

(b) *Cuando <u>no</u> estoy haciendo ejercicio me gusta <u>relajarme</u> en casa con **un libro o una revista**.*

(c) *Cada sábado **voy de compras** con mis amigas, ¡y siempre gasto mucho dinero en ropa!*

(d) *Durante la semana trabajo como **camarera**, pero no me gusta porque <u>la comida</u> es asquerosa y <u>los clientes</u> siempre se quejan.*

(e) *Sin embargo, la próxima semana voy a ir **a la playa** a pasar mis vacaciones. ¡Qué genial!*

Mark Scheme:

0-5	- Award one mark for each correct answer, up to five. - Incorrect or multiple answers score 0 marks for that question.

Tareas domésticas

4 ¿Cómo ayudan estos jóvenes en casa?	
(a) Jorge: E	[1]
(b) Luisa: D	[1]
(c) Sonia: C	[1]
(d) Carlitos: A	[1]
(e) Micaela: B	[1]

This section of dialogue occurs as one conversation, with no pauses until the end. Therefore, it's a good idea to make notes while listening to the recording.

The title suggests the core vocabulary you will need for this question: household chores. Not all of the pictures are mentioned, and they don't necessarily occur in the order that you hear them. Put a neat line through each picture when you have used it once so you can see which options remain.

TOP TIP: Make sure to listen to <u>everything</u> each person says, as this may help if you don't know the specific vocabulary.

For example, Jorge **(a)** says that, like Cai in the example, he helps outside (*fuera*) by watering the plants (*regar las plantas*) and mowing the lawn (*cortar el césped*). Even just hearing the word *plantas* would correctly suggest image **E**, which is also the only activity that takes place outdoors - apart from walking the dog, which was the example. Come back to it once you have heard the others and can be certain, but make a note in pencil to remind you.

Similarly, in **(b)**, vacuum cleaning (*pasar la aspiradora*) and getting rid of the dust (*quitar el polvo*) can only be image **D**. Then Sonia **(c)** says she has to lay the table (*poner la mesa*) before meals (image **C**), and her brother (Carlitos) clears it (*quitar [la mesa]*). Carlitos is the next voice you hear **(d)**. He confirms this, and explains that he has to collect and wash the dishes (*recoger y lavar los platos*): image **A**. Don't be thrown by the plates and cutlery in image **C** - you've already used this for Sonia - the key element is the <u>washing</u> of the dishes, not the <u>setting</u> of them. Finally, Micaela **(e)** says she is just in charge of tidying her own room (*arreglar mi propio cuarto*), which includes making the bed (*hacer la cama*): image **B**.

Once you've completed your answers, **check them**. Make sure you don't have multiple answers for a single question, or the same picture twice.

Full Transcript
M: *Yo ayudo en casa a **pasear al perro**. ¿Y tú, Jorge?*
M: *Bueno, nosotros no tenemos un perro sino un conejo. Pero yo también ayudo <u>fuera</u>. **Riego las plantas** y <u>corto el césped</u>.*
F: *¡Qué bien! Yo simplemente tengo que **pasar la aspiradora** para <u>quitar el polvo</u>. Sonia, ¿qué haces tú?*
F: *<u>Antes de comer</u>, mis padres quieren que **ponga la mesa**. Pero después, mi hermano tiene que <u>quitarla</u> y yo puedo ir a mi habitación. ¿No es verdad, Carlitos?*
M: *Sí, así es. Tengo que recoger y **lavar los platos**.*
F: *Para mí es distinto. Lo único que debo hacer es <u>arreglar mi propio cuarto</u>, o sea, **hacer la cama**.*
M: *¡Qué suerte!*

Mark Scheme:

0-5	- Award one mark for each correct answer, up to five. - Incorrect or multiple answers score 0 marks for that question.

Mi colegio

5 María Josefa habla de su asignatura favorita. ¿Qué dice?	
(a) *F*	[1]
(b) *C*	[1]
(c) *H*	[1]

Again, this recording is without pauses, so you need to listen attentively throughout and extract the relevant information when it appears. The answers are not always obvious, but they do at least occur in order. The questions are multiple choice, so you probably won't have to make copious notes.

TOP TIP: Find the possible answers first.

When a question offers several words to complete a sentence, you can apply logic to eliminate the majority of the options before you have even heard the recording. Look at what would make sense in the context of the sentence: Is it missing a verb or a noun? An adjective or adverb? If a verb is missing, which person (I, you, he/she/it, we, you plural, they)? If it's a noun, what type of noun? Could it be singular, plural, masculine, or feminine? If it's an adjective, it will have to agree with the noun, so should it end in -o/-a/-os/-as? You will then be left with only two or three options for each question.

For instance, the example question is looking for a (plural, feminine) noun, specifically a school subject, which leaves either: *B Ciencias* or *I Matemáticas*.

5(a) This question is looking for a day of the week, which leaves: *A Jueves* or *F Lunes*. María Josefa mentions both of these days, along with *miércoles*, but then says she **prefers** (*me gustan más*) classes at the beginning of the week: so Monday (**F**).

5(b) We are looking for an adjective to describe the female teacher, so the adjective will be singular and feminine - therefore the missing word is <u>likely</u> to end in -a, although not all adjectives agree like this (for example, adjectives that end in -e, like *grande*). The possible options are: *C Estricta*, *E Simpática*, or *G Gorda*. You could argue that the missing word could be a noun, such as a profession, but that would leave either the contradictory sentence *La profesora es médica*, or the redundant *La profesora es profesora*.

The actual adjective María Josefa uses is *fantástica*, which doesn't correspond to any of the options. Using *aunque* (= although), she goes on to say that Sra. Estevez makes them do their work in silence (*sin hablar* = without speaking) and that there are punishments (*castigos*). So *estricta* is the best fit (**C**).

5(c) This sentence is missing a noun to describe María Josefa's ideal job, so this is where we could use either **B** *Médica* or **H** *Profesora* - a singular, feminine noun.

Following on from the description of Sra. Estevez as strict, María Josefa changes her tone (*sin embargo*) and reveals that she is inspired to do something similar to her teacher. She **doesn't** want to go to medical school, however - this is something her **parents** want her to do.

Full Transcript
F: *Voy a un instituto donde estudiamos muchas materias distintas tales como física, química y **mi asignatura preferida, las matemáticas**. Las tenemos tres veces a la semana: el lunes, el miércoles y el jueves. Me gustan más las clases al principio de la semana, porque estamos descansados después del fin de semana. La Señora Estevez es una profesora fantástica, aunque siempre exige que hagamos las tareas sin hablar y hay castigos. Sin embargo, me inspira para hacer algo así cuando sea mayor, **aunque mis padres quieren que vaya a la facultad de medicina**.*

Mark Scheme:

0-3	- Award one mark for each correct answer, up to three. - Incorrect or multiple answers score 0 marks for that question.

El libro azul de Colombia

6 ¿Qué seis frases son correctas?	
(a) (c) (e) (f) (h) (k)	[6]

This recording is based on a longer passage, which requires you to pick out the information and compare it to the sentences in the table. Make sure you have read those sentences first! As the mark scheme suggests, there are **six** marks, one for each cross in a correct box. Check that you have exactly six answers crossed when you have reached the end of the question.

The answers occur in order in the recording, which makes it easier to keep track. Listen out for synonyms and key phrases used in the sentences.

Remember: just because a word or two from one of the sentences is said in the recording, this **does not** mean that the whole sentence is automatically true. Take everything in its context, and make notes, which you can review in the pauses - there won't be enough time to do this while you're listening.

TOP TIP: Use your time wisely.

Remember that you have five minutes before the recording to look at these questions. Use this time to underline the key words in each sentence. Make notes, or simply think of possible synonyms for these words, or other ways the recording could paraphrase them to convey the same meaning.

When you listen to the recording, your underlined words will help you focus on the key information.

For example:
(a) *El libro está lleno de imágenes.* – TRUE
(b) *El libro es monocromático.* – FALSE (= no cross needed)

Other words for *imágenes* could be *dibujos, arte, fotografías, ilustraciones* etc. and we are told there is *una gran cantidad* of these (the latter two), which is equivalent (=) to the phrase *está lleno de* (to be full of).

However, the next sentence is not true. A synonymous phrase for *monocromático* might be *en blanco y negro*, but we are in fact told that the book is printed *a todo color* (in full colour), which is contradictory (≠).

> *… contiene una gran cantidad de ilustraciones, retratos, mapas y fotografías a todo color.*

Está lleno de = una gran cantidad de
Imágenes = ilustraciones, retratos, mapas, y fotografías
Monocromático ≠ a todo color

(c) *Fue encargado por el actual presidente de Colombia.* – FALSE
(d) *Fue diseñado para promover Colombia en otros países mundiales.* – TRUE

We are told in the recording that the book was commissioned as a promotional guide to show Colombia to the rest of the world, especially (*sobre todo*) the English-speaking world. There is no trick here: this extra information is complementary, not contradictory.

However, we are also told that the commission was made in 1918, by the then president, not the current president - *actual* is a **false friend** meaning "<u>current</u>", not "actual"!

> *En pocas palabras, es <u>una guía promocional</u> de la historia de Colombia. <u>Fue encargado en 1918</u> por <u>el entonces presidente</u> José Vicente Concha para mostrar <u>al resto del mundo</u> cómo es su país, sobre todo para diferenciarlo de los países angloparlantes.*

Promover = una guía promocional
Otros países mundiales = resto del mundo, los países angloparlantes
el actual presidente ≠ el entonces presidente, en 1918

(e) *Está escrito <u>en inglés y español</u>.* – TRUE

Following on from the previous sentence concerning English-speaking countries, we learn that the book is written in both (*ambos*) languages. The *aunque* clause isn't a contradiction, but it does specifically mention the translations (*traducciones*) into English, which sometimes sound a little odd.

> *… está escrito en <u>ambos idiomas,</u> aunque a veces las traducciones al inglés suenan un poco raras.*

en inglés y español = ambos idiomas, traducciones al inglés

(f) *<u>La historia política</u> de Colombia es muy <u>turbulenta</u>.* – TRUE
(g) *Hoy en día, Colombia es un símbolo de <u>modernización</u>.* – FALSE

We are given a list of events that contributed to the unstable era (*época (muy) inestable*), such as the 1000 Days War and the Reyes dictatorship, which finally culminated in a period of peace. However, by this time the country was very out of sync with the rest of the modernised world.

> *Cuenta la historia del país después de una época muy inestable, incluida una gran guerra y la dictadura de Rafael Reyes. Al comienzo del siglo veinte empezó un período de paz en un país que estaba <u>fuera de sincronización</u> con <u>el mundo moderno</u>.*

La historia política = la historia del país
Turbulenta = inestable

Símbolo de modernización ≠ fuera de sincronización con el mundo moderno.

(h) *El Libro hace <u>mucha referencia</u> <u>al estado económico</u> del país.* – TRUE

We are told that the economy of the country is a key focus of the book, which directly correlates with the sentence we are given. To reinforce this, the resources (*recursos*) of the cities and the possible deals (*negocios*) are mentioned.

> … <u>un foco clave</u> del libro no obstante es <u>la economía del país</u>, incluso los <u>recursos</u> de sus ciudades y posibilidades de <u>negocios</u>.

Mucha referencia = un foco clave
El estado económico = la economía

(i) *Contiene música escrita por un conductor <u>colombiano famoso</u>.* – FALSE
(j) *Se celebran <u>las habilidades y logros</u> de las mujeres colombianas.* – FALSE

These are a slightly different type of "false" answer, because instead of directly contradicting the sentence, the key information isn't actually given in the recording. Sometimes you will have the option to write that the information is not mentioned, but **as you only have two options here, you must write "false".**

The musical piece is mentioned, but the composer is not given, let alone whether they were Colombian and famous. Likewise, the skills (*habilidades*) and successes (*logros*) of the featured women are not mentioned, simply their beauty.

> *Además, contiene una pieza musical y una sección famosa que muestra las "bellezas colombianas" - 50 páginas dedicadas a guapas mujeres colombianas de la época.*

(k) *<u>Muchos expertos</u> quieren comprarlo pero es <u>casi imposible</u>.* – TRUE
(l) *Sin embargo, el libro está disponible en línea.* – FALSE

Finally, we are told that a printed copy is extremely difficult to find for sale (the superlative of *difícil* is *dificilísimo*). Whether the book is available online or not is not mentioned at all.

> *Sin embargo, muchos coleccionistas han descubierto que es dificilísimo encontrar un ejemplo impreso para comprar.*

Expertos = coleccionistas
Casi imposible = dificilísimo

Full Transcript

M: ¿Has oído hablar del "Libro azul de Colombia"? Se llama así por la cubierta azul con título dorado, contiene una gran cantidad de ilustraciones, retratos, mapas y fotografías a todo color. En pocas palabras, es una guía promocional de la historia de Colombia. Fue encargado en 1918 por el entonces presidente José Vicente Concha para mostrar al resto del mundo cómo es su país, sobre todo para diferenciarlo de los países angloparlantes. No obstante, está escrito en ambos idiomas, aunque a veces las traducciones al inglés suenan un poco raro.

Cuenta la historia del país después de una época muy inestable, incluida una gran guerra y la dictadura de Rafael Reyes. Al comienzo del siglo veinte empezó un período de paz en un país que estaba fuera de sincronización con el mundo moderno. Sin puertos, ni infraestructura, un foco clave del libro no obstante es la economía del país, incluso los recursos de sus ciudades y posibilidades de negocios. Además, contiene una pieza musical y una sección famosa que muestra las "bellezas colombianas" – 50 páginas dedicadas a guapas mujeres colombianas de la época. A pesar de, o gracias a, todas estas peculiaridades editoriales, queda claro que el "Libro azul" es una joya de información cultural idiosincrásica. Sin embargo, muchos coleccionistas han descubierto que es dificilísimo encontrar un ejemplo impreso para comprar.

Mark Scheme:

0-6	- Award one mark for each correct answer, up to six. - Deduct one mark for each incorrect answer, even if the correct answers are also crossed.

Entrevista con una actriz

> **7 (a) How does she describe the director?**
>
> *The best thing (that can happen to you if you want to work in the industry)*
> OR:
> *Her idol* [1]

Longer passages like this are designed to help the strongest candidates achieve top grades, and may contain unfamiliar words or terms. If you don't understand something that you hear, try and work it out from the context.

TOP TIP: Make shorthand notes.

It is impossible to write everything down. Make shorthand notes or only write down key words. For example, the answer to **7(a)**, "The best thing that can happen to you if you want to work in the industry", is long, and by the time you've written that, the recording will have moved on. Writing something like "Best, want wk industry" in the answer space allows you to quickly move on to the next question; you can return to it during the pauses or at the end of the listening section to write it out in full. (Alternatively, she says that he is her "idol", which also would gain you the mark.)

Use the spaces on the question paper to make notes, but put your shorthand responses in the answer spaces to help you quickly remember the question, and also to prevent you from writing in the wrong section when you return to it.

The relevant information comes right at the start of the piece:

Acabo de trabajar con un director que <u>es mi ídolo</u>. Trabajar con él fue lo mejor, <u>lo mejor que te puede pasar</u> si quieres trabajar en esta industria ...

Remember to answer in English. Be specific with your translations, as roughly paraphrasing might not be enough to get you the mark. For example: "She loved it" or "It was brilliant" isn't acceptable as an answer, as it sounds like guesswork. This applies to all the answers.

Mark Scheme:

0/1	- Candidate has not identified the important information in the passage. - Candidate's translation is nonspecific, indicating guesswork.
1/1	- Candidate has identified and supplied the correct information.

---

7 (b) (i) Give two things that she admires about the director.

Any TWO of:
> *His sense of humour*
> *His (unlimited) patience*
> *His imagination*
> *The characters he creates*
> *His workrate/he is a workaholic.* [2]

The speaker gives a lot of information for this answer, so you have to be alert in order to pick out the key words or phrases that will score you a point. Again, writing down **everything** you hear would be next to impossible and a waste of time, because not all of it is relevant to answering the question.

TOP TIP: Write out words you don't know.

Get used to trying to work out words which you don't know when you hear them. Write them down as accurately as you can on a spare bit of the page, and see if they look similar to another word, either in Spanish or in English: they may share a common root. For example, *paciencia* or *humor* might sound different to their English equivalents when spoken, but they look very similar written down.

Tiene un <u>sentido del humor</u> maravilloso, <u>paciencia</u> ilimitada y una <u>imaginación</u> que te deja <u>crear un personaje</u> tan real y orgánico que se queda contigo para siempre. Es más, es un <u>adicto al trabajo</u> …

Any of this information is acceptable as an answer (give TWO points). Again, make sure your translations are specific and directly relevant to the question. Repeating information from the first answer, e.g. that working with him is a gift and a pleasure, would be too vague. Also remember that you are required to give two **separate** pieces of information to get full marks: writing "creating real and organic characters that stay with you forever" is only one point and therefore only scores one mark.

Mark Scheme:

0/2	- No relevant information supplied.
1/2	- Candidate has identified **one** thing that she admires the director for.
2/2	- Candidate has identified **two** separate things that she admires him for.

---

7 (b) (ii) Why does she compare him to a spider?

He is a workaholic.
OR:
He juggles/connects a lot of things (in his mind/as if he had eight legs).   [1]

This follow-up question involves interpreting the imagery that she uses: that the director seems <u>like</u> a spider (*araña*) because of his work-rate, able to reach out and connect diverse ideas together, as if he had eight long legs. It is important to understand her use of simile: she is not saying he actually has eight legs (*patas* is used instead of *piernas* when referring to animal limbs)! The extra bit of information about his awareness and keenness to learn isn't relevant.

> *Es más, es un adicto al trabajo y, debido a que es consciente de todo, <u>puede conectar un montón de cosas</u> en su mente. Es <u>como una araña</u> con ocho patas largas, <u>extendiéndose y conectando muchas ideas diversas</u>.*

Mark Scheme:

0/1	- Information is not supplied or not relevant.
1/1	- Candidate has identified and supplied the correct information, and has interpreted the intention of the simile (even if only implicitly - e.g. "hard-working").

---

7 (c) What was her reaction to the film they worked on? Give two ideas.

Any TWO of:
A revelation
She cried/cries every time
Surprised
She understands the film's appreciation for love   [2]

Similar to question **7(b)(i)**, there is a lot of information given and you are required to pick out the key words. You are asked to find a **reaction**, so words that indicate an emotional response, as well as any adjectives she uses, are relevant. You can write down what she said as reported speech, e.g. she thinks it is "a revelation", or give this information entirely as a quote, remembering to use quotation marks, e.g. "I cry every time I see it".

> *¿En cuanto a la película? Pues es <u>una revelación</u>. <u>Lloro cada vez</u> que la veo, y sigo <u>sorprendida</u> por su humanidad y humor …*

Mark Scheme:

0/2	- No relevant information supplied.
1/2	- Candidate has identified **one** thing that indicates her reaction to the film. Reported speech is acceptable.
2/2	- Candidate has identified **two** separate things that indicate her reaction to the film, including reported speech.

7 (d) What is the message of the film, according to her?

The love of life
OR:
Love   [1]

The speaker supplies a fairly straightforward answer to this question, by explicitly saying what the *mensaje principal* of the film is: the love of life. Any answer mentioning "the love of her life" would be incorrect. The fact that the film also explores the themes of families and identity isn't relevant.

> *Tiene que ver con la familia y la identidad, pero <u>su mensaje es el amor a la vida</u>. La entiendo de una manera muy profunda …*

Mark Scheme:

0/1	- Information is not supplied or not relevant.
1/1	- Candidate has identified and supplied the correct information, concerning the **message** of the film, not her personal reaction.

7 (e) What personal reason does she give for why this film is so special to her?

She was going through a divorce   [1]

The speaker concludes by naming her divorce as a personal (rather than professional) reason why the film is so meaningful for her, because it helped her to understand why people do what they do in the name of love. You may give this explanation, but mentioning her divorce is essential to getting the mark.

The information for these final few questions (from **7(c)** to **7(e)**) occurs very close together towards the end of the recording. This highlights the need to take brief notes while listening to the recording. Writing too much may cause you to miss vital information.

> *La entiendo de una manera muy profunda porque en ese momento <u>me estaba divorciando</u> y esa película me ayudó a entender por qué hacemos lo que hacemos en nombre del amor.*

Mark Scheme:

0/1	- Information is not supplied or not relevant.
1/1	- Candidate has identified and supplied the correct information, citing her divorce as the personal reason.

Full Transcript

F: *Acabo de trabajar con un director que es mi ídolo. Trabajar con él fue lo mejor, lo mejor que te puede pasar si quieres trabajar en esta industria. Tiene un sentido del humor maravilloso, paciencia ilimitada, y una imaginación que te deja crear un personaje tan real y orgánico que se queda contigo para siempre. Es más, es un adicto al trabajo y, debido a que es consciente de todo, puede conectar un montón de cosas en su mente. Es como una araña de ocho patas largas, extendiéndose y conectando muchas ideas diversas.*

¿En cuanto a la película? Pues es una revelación. Lloro cada vez que la veo, y sigo sorprendida por su humanidad y humor. Tiene que ver con la familia y la identidad, pero su mensaje principal es el amor a la vida. La entiendo de una manera muy profunda porque en ese momento me estaba divorciando y esa película me ayudó a entender por qué hacemos lo que hacemos en nombre del amor.

¿Universidad o no?

8 Razones para ir a la universidad

Any THREE of these, in any order:
Conseguir un buen trabajo
OR:
Ganar más/tener un sueldo muy bueno [1]

Te da habilidades/técnicas transferibles
OR:
Te prepara para muchas ocupaciones distintas [1]

Eliges los cursos que te interesan [1]

No tienes que especializarte tan temprano [1]

Puedes trabajar con académicos apasionados [1]

Razones para no ir a la universidad

Any THREE of these, in any order:
Cuesta demasiado
OR:
Es demasiado cara
OR:
No tener suficiente dinero [1]

No garantiza/Muy difícil encontrar un trabajo
OR:
La tasa de desempleo es peor entre los graduados
OR:
Demasiados graduados y pocos puestos [1]

Mejor hacer un aprendizaje o formación profesional
OR:
(Un aprendizaje/formación profesional) no cuesta tanto [1]

Es aburrido estudiar más [1]

[Maximum 6]

This is another long passage of dialogue, so the best method will be to make shorthand notes throughout and then fill the gaps in your notes during a pause – see *TOP TIP: Make shorthand notes* in this paper, **Question 7(a)**. Listen as best as you can, and try and piece the meaning together from the context. For example, hearing the words *trabajo* and *sueldo* close together might lead you to the argument that a university degree leads to a good job with a good wage (one mark). To save time, you could simply write *trabajo* and then fill in the rest of the sentence later, in the pause. Remember, you don't have to write in full sentences.

The dialogue is in the form of a discussion, or argument, and you have to judge which assertions are <u>positive reasons</u> for going to university, and which support <u>not going</u>. They don't necessarily occur in an ABAB order - there might be two negatives given in the same sentence. However, make sure that the reasons you give are different: *cuesta demasiado* and *no tener suficiente dinero* make the same point and so would only gain one mark.

TOP TIP: Look for opinions.

Look out for words or phrase that introduce **opinions**, such as *en mi opinión, según yo, a mi parecer, pienso/creo/opino que* etc., or a **counter-argument**, such as *pero, sin embargo, no obstante, (no) estoy de acuerdo, (no) es verdad* etc.

Clue words/phrases in the following transcript are <u>underlined</u> and answers are in **bold**.

Full Transcript

F: *¡Hola Jaime! Me dijo tu madre que estás pensando en no ir a la universidad el año que viene. Pero, ¿por qué no? Es un lugar excelente donde puedes **conocer a mucha gente nueva**.*

M: *Sí, así es. <u>En mi opinión</u> **cuesta demasiado** y **no me alcanza el dinero**.*

F: *Claro, <u>pero</u> <u>me parece que</u> cuando salgas de la Universidad serás graduado y podrás **conseguir un buen trabajo** con **un sueldo muy bueno**.*

M: *<u>No es verdad</u>. Hay mucha gente que no puede encontrar un trabajo después de la universidad porque **no hay suficientes puestos de trabajo**. La tasa de desempleo es peor entre los graduados jóvenes, porque **hay demasiados graduados y pocos puestos**. <u>Mejor hacer un aprendizaje o formación profesional</u> para tener habilidades útiles para el mundo del trabajo. Y esta opción **no es tan cara**.*

F: *<u>Sin embargo</u>, la universidad te da **habilidades y técnicas transferibles**. O sea, **te prepara para muchas ocupaciones distintas**, y **no tienes que especializarte tan temprano**. <u>Además</u>, puedes **elegir los cursos** que más te interesan y te inspiran, y puedes **trabajar con académicos tan apasionados** y entusiasmados como tú. Yo muero de ganas de ir.*

M: *Bien por ti. <u>Pero</u> <u>me parece</u> **muy aburrido** estudiar más cuando puedo trabajar. Creo que nunca vamos a estar de acuerdo.*

Mark Scheme:

0-6	- Award one mark for each correct answer, up to six. - Each answer must contain clearly separate information or reasons, not repeat the same point in different words. - Incorrect or repeated answers do not score.

Regreso de Argentina

9 (a) (i) ¿Cuánto tiempo llevaba en Argentina?
(Más de) nueve meses/casi diez meses. [1]
(ii) ¿Por qué ha vuelto ahora?
Para visitar a su abuela OR: *Su abuela está (muy) enferma.* [1]

TOP TIP: Be specific.

Full sentences aren't usually necessary **in listening papers** (unless otherwise stated in the question). You are being marked on your comprehension skills, so be succinct and precise in your answers. Providing too much information is a waste of time, and may hide your main answer from the examiner.

As the recording says she has been away for <u>almost</u> ten months, there is more than one way of phrasing a correct answer to **(i)**.

For **(ii)**, you do need to show that you have understood the context of her visit: her ill grandmother (your core vocabulary is important here).

*Acabo de volver de Argentina después de **casi diez meses** para **visitar a mi abuela** que **está muy enferma**.*

Mark Scheme:

0/2	- Information is not supplied or not relevant.
1/2	- Candidate has identified and supplied the correct information for one half of the question only.
2/2	- Candidate has identified and supplied the correct information for both halves of the question.

(b) (i) A tu amiga, ¿qué aspectos de Argentina le gustan? Da dos ideas.

Any TWO of:
La comida/carne (fantástica)
La gente es simpática
El tiempo/siempre hace sol   [2]

(ii) ¿Qué es que no le gusta?

(A veces/en el verano) puede hacer/hace demasiado calor   [1]

In the first half of this question, you simply have to pick two aspects of Argentinian life that she enjoyed, so look out for positive adjectives, qualifying adverbs such as *muy* and *tan*, and superlatives (see **Steps to a Higher Grade**). Your answers do need to address the question directly, so simply stating (*piensa que*) *es increíble*, whilst a positive description, is **not** specific enough to gain a mark.

The information required also carries on to the next part of the recording, in which she both compliments the weather and complains about it. Again, look out for qualifying adverbs such as *mucho* and *muy,* which can be either positive or negative, and *demasiado* (<u>too</u> much/many), which is almost always used negatively – too much of anything is a bad thing!

A vague answer to the second part of the question would be *"los meses de verano"*. This wouldn't score a mark because it doesn't specifically address **what** exactly she doesn't like about the summer months (the heat).

Es <u>increíble</u> aquello, de verdad. **La comida es <u>fantástica</u>**, *especialmente* **la carne**, *y* **la gente es <u>muy simpática</u>**. *Además, siempre* **hace <u>mucho</u> sol** *que* <u>*me encanta*</u>, <u>*pero*</u> *la verdad es que a veces* **puede hacer <u>demasiado</u> calor** *para mí, sobre todo durante* **los meses de verano.**

Mark Scheme:

0/3	- No information supplied or information is not relevant.
1/3	- Candidate has only identified and supplied one correct aspect out of three (either positive or negative) about life in Argentina between the two halves of the question.
2/3	- Candidate has identified and supplied two correct aspects out of three (either positive or negative) about life in Argentina between the two halves of the question.
3/3	- Candidate has identified and supplied the correct information for both halves of the question: two specific and separate positive aspects of life in Argentina, followed by one negative aspect.

(c) Da dos consejos para ir a Argentina.

Any TWO of:

Llevar una botella de agua.
Estar vigilante cuando visitas ciudades grandes/ciertos lugares pueden ser peligrosos.
Aprender un poco de español. [2]

This is another question where a lot of information is given at once. You have to take notes sensibly and then fill in the blanks during the pauses. The question is asking for advice, so look out for words such as *consejo/aconsejar, esencial, vital, necesario, imprescindible* and *mejor*. The reasons for the advice are not needed. Also look out for linking words and conjunctions such as *y, también, además (de)* etc., which connect separate ideas.

---

*<u>Es imprescindible</u> **llevar contigo una botella de agua** si <u>vas a visitar Argentina</u>.*
*También si vas a ir a las ciudades grandes, <u>te pido</u> **que estés vigilante** y atento porque puede ser un poco peligroso en ciertos lugares. Y <u>te aconsejo </u>que **aprendas un poco la lengua** porque mucha de la población no habla bien inglés.*

Mark Scheme:

0/2	- Information is not supplied or not relevant.
1/2	- Candidate has identified and supplied one piece of advice for travelling to Argentina. - Repeated or incorrect answers do not score.
2/2	- Candidate has identified and supplied **two** separate pieces of advice.

(d) ¿Qué perdió su amiga en Buenos Aires?

Su bolso
OR:
Su pasaporte [1]

This fairly simple question might throw up some confusion, because she does in fact mention two things her friend lost, as her passport was inside her bag. However, either or both pieces of information would gain you the mark.

The extra bits of information outlined above are relevant to the question, so if you have understood them, there is no harm in writing them down now. However, information such as that they never found the bag again, or that it happened during her first month, is extraneous information, so don't write that.

---

*Cuando fuimos a Buenos Aires en el primer mes, mi amiga **perdió el bolso** con **su pasaporte** y nunca lo encontramos.*

Mark Scheme:

0/1	- No information supplied or information is not relevant.
1/1	- Candidate has only identified and supplied one correct item that her friend has lost. - Mentioning both her passport and her bag, or either, scores full marks. - Deduct a mark for an incorrect answer, or guesswork, even if the correct answer if also supplied.

(e) ¿Le gustaría volver a Argentina en el futuro? ¿Por qué/por qué no?

Sí   [1]

Tiene novio/está enamorada/ha encontrado a un chico argentino.   [1]

This is a two-part question, and requires you to interpret her reasons (*porque*) for wanting to return to Argentina when possible. Don't be thrown by the *aunque* - this introduces information that isn't relevant to the question. The specific answer is that she has met and fallen in love with a boy there.

<u>Tengo planes de regresar</u> cuando sea posible, aunque solo cuando sepa la situación de mi abuelita. Sobre todo <u>porque</u> **he conocido a un chico argentino muy lindo***... <u>Qué romántico</u>, ¿no?*

Mark Scheme:

0/2	- Information is not supplied or not relevant.
1/2	- Correct answer ("Yes") supplied, but no or incorrect reason given.
2/2	- Correct answer ("Yes") and correct reason supplied.

Full transcript

F: *¡Hola! Acabo de volver de Argentina después de casi diez meses para visitar a mi abuela que está muy enferma. Es increíble aquello, de verdad. La comida es fantástica, especialmente la carne, y la gente es muy simpática. Además, siempre hace mucho sol que me encanta, pero la verdad es que a veces puede hacer demasiado calor para mí, sobre todo durante los meses de verano.*

Es imprescindible llevar contigo una botella de agua si vas a visitar Argentina. También si vas a ir a las ciudades grandes, te pido que estés vigilante y atento porque puede ser un poco peligroso en ciertos lugares. Y te aconsejo que aprendas un poco la lengua porque mucha de la población no habla bien inglés. Cuando fuimos a Buenos Aires en el primer mes, mi amiga perdió el bolso con su pasaporte y nunca lo encontramos.

Tengo planes de regresar cuando sea posible, aunque solo cuando sepa la situación de mi abuelita. Sobre todo, porque he encontrado a un chico argentino muy lindo. Solo nos conocemos desde hace seis meses, pero queremos casarnos en el futuro. Qué romántico, ¿no?

END OF SOLUTIONS FOR PAPER 1

Listening Paper 2

Visit www.rsleducational.co.uk/spanishaudio to download the audio file for this paper.

If you wish to complete this paper in timed conditions, allow 45 minutes plus 5 minutes' reading time.

Instructions

- Use **black** ink or ballpoint pen.
- Answer **all** questions.
- Answer the questions in the spaces provided.
  - *There may be more space than you require.*
- Dictionaries are **not** allowed.

Advice

- You have 5 minutes to read through the paper before the recording starts.
- You will hear each extract twice. You may write at any time during the examination. There will be a pause between each question.
- Read each question **carefully** before attempting it.
- The marks available for each question are given in [square brackets]. These give you an indication of how long to spend on each question.
- There is a total of **50 marks** available for this paper.
- Leave time to check your answers at the end, if possible.

Answer ALL questions.

Reciclaje

1 ¿Qué **cuatro** productos se pueden reciclar? Pon una equis **[X]** en cada casilla correcta.

Which **four** products can be recycled? Put a cross **[X]** in each correct box.

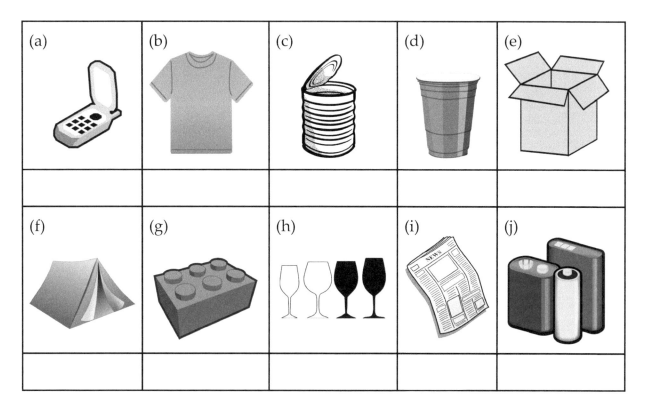

(Total for Question 1 = 4 marks)

Valencia

2   Llegas a Valencia y buscas ayuda. Pon una equis [X] en cada casilla correcta.

You arrive in Valencia and ask for help. Put a cross [X] in each correct box.

(a) ¿Qué número de autobús va al centro de la ciudad?

(i)	(ii)	(iii)
26	62	6

(b) ¿Dónde puedes comprar un mapa?

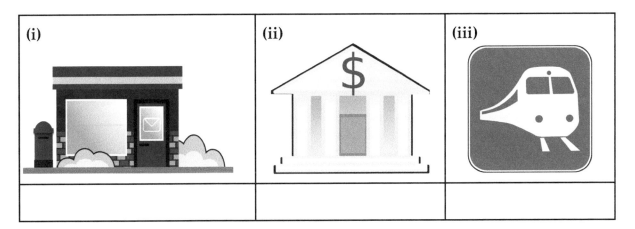

(i)	(ii)	(iii)

(c) ¿Qué puedes hacer esta noche?

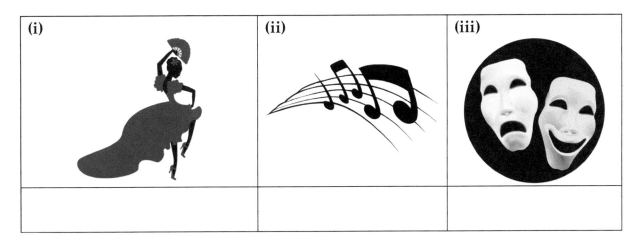

(i)	(ii)	(iii)

(d) ¿Qué vas a hacer mañana?

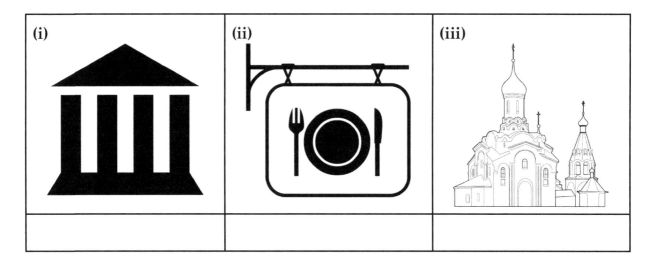

(e) ¿Dónde está tu hotel?

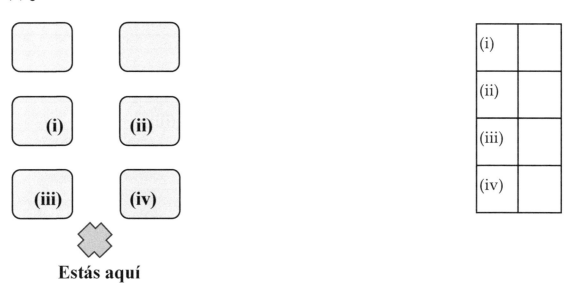

(i)	
(ii)	
(iii)	
(iv)	

(Total for Question 2 = 5 marks)

Deportes

3   Paco habla sobre los deportes que hace. Escucha la grabación y contesta las preguntas que están debajo. Pon una equis [X] en cada casilla correcta.

Paco is talking about the sports that he does. Listen to the recording and answer the questions below. Put a cross [X] in each correct box.

(a) What sport does Paco want to play professionally?

(i) **Football**	
(ii) **Golf**	
(iii) **Running**	
(iv) **Weightlifting**	

(b) How long has he been playing?

(i) **10 years**	
(ii) **7 years**	
(iii) **17 years**	
(iv) **7 months**	

(c) At what time does he like to go to the gym?

(i) **15:00**	
(ii) **15:30**	
(iii) **17:00**	
(iv) **08:00**	

(d) Who inspired him to start playing the sport?

(i) **His mother**	
(ii) **His father**	
(iii) **His grandfather**	
(iv) **His uncle**	

(e) What is his favourite position?

(i) **Goalkeeper**	
(ii) **Defender**	
(iii) **Midfielder**	
(iv) **Forward**	

(f) When is the next match?

(i) **In two weeks**	
(ii) **This weekend**	
(iii) **Next year**	
(iv) **None of the above**	

(Total for Question 3 = 6 marks)

Una dieta equilibrada

4   Escucha esta entrevista con una nutricionista. Luego, pon la(s) letra(s) adecuada(s) en cada casilla para indicar si las afirmaciones son verdaderas, falsas o si no se mencionan.

Listen to this interview with a dietician. Then put the appropriate letter(s) in each box to indicate whether the information is true, false, or not mentioned.

Verdadero = V
Falso = F
No se menciona = NM

Ejemplo: Es importantísimo tener una dieta equilibrada.	V
(a) Muchas personas planean sus comidas.	
(b) Las grasas no son saludables.	
(c) Es esencial tener comida fresca en casa.	
(d) Los productos que contienen leche son importantes para la salud.	
(e) Los vegetarianos son demasiado perezosos para cocinar.	
(f) Es más económico comer comida rápida.	
(g) Necesitas comer comida caliente tres veces al día.	
(h) Si no estás seguro, debes pedir consejo a un experto.	

(Total for Question 4 = 8 marks)

Informes

5   Escucha estos informes y escribe **lo que** ha pasado y **dónde**. Contesta **en inglés.**

Listen to these reports and write **what** has happened and **where.** Answer **in English.**

(a)

Event	Place
Ejemplo: Robbery	

(b)

Event	Place

(c)

Event	Place

(d)

Event	Place

(Total for Question 5 = 7 marks)

El mundo del trabajo

6   Estas personas hablan sobre sus empleos. Escucha lo que dicen y escribe **en español** los aspectos positivos y los aspectos negativos de cada trabajo.

These people are talking about their jobs. Listen to what they say and write down **in Spanish** the positive and the negative aspects of each job.

(a)

Positivo	Negativo
	Ejemplo: Largas horas

(b)

Positivo	Negativo

(c)

Positivo	Negativo

(Total for Question 6 = 5 marks)

Bolsas de plástico

7   Escucha esta grabación sobre un supermercado. Luego, contesta las preguntas que están debajo **en inglés**.

Listen to this recording about a supermarket. Then answer the questions below **in English**.

(a) When does this change come into effect?   [1]

……………………………………………………………………………………………

(b) What are the two new options?   [2]

……………………………………………………………………………………………

……………………………………………………………………………………………

(c) What happens if your bag is damaged?   [1]

……………………………………………………………………………………………

(d) What effect does the supermarket think this change will have? Give **two** ideas.
                                                                           [2]

……………………………………………………………………………………………

……………………………………………………………………………………………

(e) Who is this good news for, according to the government?   [1]

……………………………………………………………………………………………

(f) Who does this news **not** affect?   [1]

……………………………………………………………………………………………

(g) What does the supermarket now hope will happen?   [1]

……………………………………………………………………………………………

(Total for Question 7 = 9 marks)

Entrevista a un escritor

8   Escucha esta entrevista a un escritor conocido y luego contesta las preguntas que están debajo **en español**. No tienes que escribir frases completas.

Listen to this interview with a well-known writer, and then answer the questions below **in Spanish**. You don't have to write in full sentences.

(a) ¿De qué género es su nuevo libro?   [1]

....

(b) ¿Qué le inspira para escribir? Da **dos** ideas.   [2]

....

....

....

(c) Según él, ¿qué responsabilidad tiene un escritor?   [1]

....

(d) ¿Qué consejos tiene para los escritores jóvenes? Menciona **dos** ideas.   [2]

....

....

....

(Total for Question 8 = 6 marks)

TOTAL FOR PAPER = 50 MARKS

Listening Paper 2 – SOLUTIONS

Reciclaje

---

1 ¿Qué cuatro productos se pueden reciclar?

> *(b) (c) (e) (i)*   [4]

This "warm-up" question tests some fairly simple core GCSE vocabulary to do with recycling (always look at the title of the question, if given). You can see at the bottom of the page that there are four marks available: one per correct answer. You are required to put a cross underneath the pictures once you hear the corresponding Spanish word(s) in the recording. Double-check after completing this question that you have crossed exactly four boxes – no more, no fewer.

Don't guess too early! Of course, many of the items pictured can actually be recycled, but you must base your answer on the information in this recording. When you read through the question for the first time, have in mind the words that may occur, and what the examiners may be testing.

You may find it helpful to put a neat line through the pictures you have already used, as well as the pictures that you can rule out as definitely incorrect, having listened to the recording. The answers won't necessarily occur in the same order as the pictures, and there are even some items mentioned that don't have a corresponding picture.

For example, you are told that there are shops where you can donate clothes and shoes (*ropa y zapatos*). There isn't a corresponding image for shoes, and the only item of clothing pictured is a T-shirt **(b)**. (Be careful too that you understand from the context that *tiendas* refers to the shops and not to tents).

Similarly, there is a special container for *latas y botellas de vidrio*. Picture **(c)** is of a can, but there are no pictures of glass bottles. There are wine glasses **(h)**, but this would be an incorrect inference. The key information is given explicitly, as is usual for these simpler questions. If you had made this mistake and put a cross under **(h)**, you would have been left with too many crosses by the end of the passage, in which case you could have deleted this answer after understanding the next section. When this happens, put a neat line through your old answer (**X**), so the examiner knows not to count it.

Plastic cannot be recycled, according to this recording, which rules out plastic cups **(d)** and Lego **(g)**, but cardboard and paper can. The corresponding images are of a cardboard box *(carton)* **(e)** and a newspaper *(periódico)* **(i)**.

Full Transcript – correct answers are given in **bold**.

F: *En nuestra ciudad se recicla mucho. Es decir, hay tiendas donde puedes donar* **ropa** *y zapatos. Las* **latas** *y botellas de vidrio van a un contenedor especial al final de la calle. En este momento, no se puede reciclar el plástico, pero el papel y el* **carton** *sí, o sea, revistas,* **periódicos** *y libros.*

Mark Scheme:

0-4	- Award one mark for each correct answer, up to four. - Deduct one mark for each incorrect answer, even if the correct answers are also crossed. *- Therefore, crossing eight boxes would mean four wrong answers and score 0 marks.*

Valencia

2 (a) ¿Qué número de autobús va al centro de la ciudad?
(iii) [1]

This section is once again testing core vocabulary, as well as your ability to listen carefully and pinpoint the key information. For **2(a)**, the correct answer (bus number six) is mentioned at the end of the sentence.

Once you have completed all parts of Question 2, **check your answers**. Make sure you have answered each question, and that you don't have multiple answers for a single one. If you have, erase or put a neat line through the wrong answer, **✗**, to signal to the examiner that you have changed your mind.

2 (b) ¿Dónde puedes comprar un mapa?
(i) [1]

In this question we are told that the post office is opposite the bank. Don't just cross *(iii)* because you hear the word *banco*, as this isn't relevant: you want to go to the **post office** to buy a map.

---

2 (c) ¿Qué puedes hacer esta noche?

   (ii)   [1]

Similarly, we are told explicitly that the free show is dedicated to Spanish music (*espectáculo de música española*). Listen to the entire context: wrongly inferring that it is a theatre or flamenco show because you hear the words *espectáculo* or *española* would lead you to the wrong answer.

---

2 (d) ¿Qué vas a hacer mañana?

   (iii)   [1]

There will be an official tour guide present in the historical buildings of the city; the cathedral is explicitly mentioned as part of this.

---

2 (e) ¿Dónde está tu hotel?

   (i)   [1]

To answer this question, you need to be able to follow basic directions in Spanish: the second street on the left (*izquierda*).

Full Transcript

(a) F: *Para ir al centro desde aquí necesitas tomar el autobús número* **seis**.
(b) *Puedes comprar un mapa* **en la oficina de correos** *que está enfrente del banco.*
(c) *Esta noche hay un* **espectáculo de música** *española en la plaza, y es completamente gratis.*
(d) *Mañana habrá un guía oficial en los edificios históricos de la ciudad, tales como* **la catedral**.
(e) *El hotel está muy cerca de aquí. Toma* **la segunda calle a la izquierda**.

Mark Scheme:

0-5	- Award one mark for each correct answer. - Multiple answers or unanswered questions score zero marks for that question.

Deportes

> **3 (a) What sport does Paco want to play professionally?**
>
>   *(i) Football*   [1]

The questions from this point on start to get a little trickier, and you need to be wary of traps – see *TOP TIP: Pay attention to the whole sentence* (**Listening Paper 1**, **Question 2**). This opening question, however, is straightforward:

> *… me gusta ser muy activo.* ***Quiero ser futbolista profesional*** *cuando sea mayor. Entreno mucho …*

> **3 (b) How long has he been playing?**
>
>   *(i) 10 years*   [1]

Rather than giving the exact answer we require, Paco tells us that he <u>began</u> training when he was seven years old, using the past tense. If he had said directly how long he had been playing, he would have used the present tense and either a construction with either *desde hace* or *llevar* + present participle e.g. *juego desde hace __ años* or *llevo __ años jugando.*

As he has already told us at the beginning of the recording that he is now seventeen, simple arithmetic will give you the correct answer of **(i) 10 years**. (*9 years* is also a mathematically possible answer, but it doesn't appear as one of the options.)

> *Entreno mucho, cinco veces a la semana, y* ***empecé cuando tenía 7 años.***

> **3 (c) At what time does he like to go to the gym?**
>
>   *(iv) 08:00*   [1]

There is a further trick in this question: Paco begins by saying he <u>used</u> to go to the gym after school (at four o'clock). Note that he has to use the imperfect tense to express this. Then he says he <u>now</u> prefers to go in the morning: **(iv)** is the only option that is before lunchtime.

> *Cuando era más joven iba al gimnasio después del colegio, o sea a las cuatro, pero hoy en día encuentro mejor el ir* ***por la mañana.***

3 (d) Who inspired him to start playing this sport?

> *(iii) His grandfather*   [1]

Abuelo is a core GCSE word, meaning "grandfather". He also clarifies that it is his grandfather on his mother's side who got him passionate about football – don't be thrown by the mention of other relatives.

> *Me apasiona el fútbol porque **mi abuelo**, el padre de mi mamá, era portero del equipo nacional hace cuarenta años. Es mi inspiración.*

3 (e) What is his favourite position?

> *(iv) Forward*   [1]

Paco's <u>grandfather</u> was an international goalkeeper (*portero*) but Paco prefers playing as a forward (*delantero*). There is another opportunity to get the correct answer if you didn't know this word: he loves to score goals (*marcar goles*).

> *Sin embargo, yo prefiero jugar como **delantero** porque me encanta **marcar goles.***

3 (f) When is the next match?

> *(ii) This weekend*   [1]

Finally, he says that they have a match this weekend (*finde* is short for *fin de semana*). The rest of the information – that they lost in the cup two weeks ago, or that it is the last match of the season – isn't relevant, so don't be distracted by it.

> ***Este finde**, tenemos un partido contra el equipo rival …*

Full Transcript
M: *Hola, yo soy Paco y **tengo 17 años**. Tengo muchos pasatiempos, y me gusta ser muy activo. **Quiero ser futbolista profesional** cuando sea mayor. Entreno mucho, cinco veces a la semana, y **empecé cuando tenía 7 años**. Cuando era más joven iba al gimnasio después del colegio, o sea a las cuatro, pero hoy en día encuentro mejor el ir **por la mañana**. Me apasiona el fútbol porque **mi abuelo**, el padre de mi mamá, era portero del equipo nacional hace cuarenta años. Es mi inspiración. Sin embargo, yo prefiero jugar como **delantero** porque me encanta marcar goles. **Este finde**, tenemos un partido contra el equipo rival, y es*

importantísimo ganar, porque perdimos contra ellos en la copa hace dos semanas y, además, es el último partido del año.

Mark Scheme:

0-6	- Award one mark for each correct answer. - Multiple answers for one question, or unanswered questions, score **zero** marks for that question.

Una dieta equilibrada

4 (a) Muchas personas planean sus comidas.
   V (Verdadero) [1]
 	
(b) Las grasas no son saludables.
   F (Falso) [1]
 	
(c) Es esencial tener comida fresca en casa.
   V [1]
 	
(d) Los productos que contienen leche son importantes para la salud.
   V [1]
 	
(e) Los vegetarianos son demasiado perezosos para cocinar.
   NM (No se menciona) [1]
 	
(f) Es más económico comer comida rápida.
   F [1]
 	
(g) Necesitas comer comida caliente tres veces al día.
   NM [1]
 	
(h) Si no estás seguro, debes pedir consejo a un experto.
   V [1]

Make sure you have read the sentences below the question first, as the recording is from a long passage. Reading the sentences for the first time while also trying to listen would be too much.

TOP TIP: Make notes in the spaces provided.

When the recording starts, you have to compare the information it gives to the sentences below. Make notes as you go along in the spaces on the question paper, and underline the key parts of the sentences. The answers will occur in the recording in order, which will help you to keep track. Review your notes in the pauses and use them to answer the questions.

(Don't write in the margins – these are for the examiners.)

Listen out for synonyms and key phrases from the sentences, as the recording is unlikely to use exactly the same form of words. Similarly, just because a word or two from the sentences is said in the recording, this does not make that entire sentence automatically true. Make sure to take everything in its context and apply logic.

In **(a)**, *muchas personas* is a direct equivalent of *mucha gente*, and *planear sus comidas* is also synonymous with *escribir un plan de comidas*. However, we are then told that all food groups, including fats (*grasas*), are necessary for a healthy diet, so **(b)** is false.

Then we are told it is *vital* (= *esencial*) that you have *ingredientes frescos* (= *comida fresca*) at home, including dairy products (*lácteos*) such as *yogur y leche* (= *productos que contienen leche*). So **(c)** and **(d)** are both true. Despite the reference to vegetarians, whether or not they are too lazy to cook **(e)** is not mentioned.

Cooking at home is much healthier than buying fast food or pre-prepared food every day, as well as being *más barato* (= *más económico*) **(f)**. Although the advice is to eat regularly, at least three times a day, it is not mentioned whether the meals need to be hot **(g)**. Finally, if you have any doubts (*si tienes alguna duda* = *si no estás seguro*), then you should speak to *un médico o un nutricionista profesional* (= *un experto*).

Full transcript
F: *Mucha gente olvida que es esencial tener una dieta equilibrada. Mucha gente encuentra útil* <u>*escribir un plan de comidas*</u> *para asegurar que su dieta es sana. Se puede organizar lo que se come durante el día, además de ver si contiene todos* <u>*los grupos esenciales,*</u> *o sea carbohidratos, proteínas, vitaminas y* <u>*grasas.*</u> *También es vital tener muchos* <u>*ingredientes frescos*</u> *en casa, como verduras,* <u>*lácteos tales como yogur y leche*</u>*, y carnes, a menos que seas vegetariano. Si estás muy ocupado, puedes cocinar y llevar el almuerzo contigo el próximo día, o guardarlo en el congelador. Es mucho más sano que comprar comida rápida o precocinada cada día, además de ser* <u>*más barato*</u>*. Come con regularidad, por lo menos tres veces al día, o sea cada tres a cinco horas, y bebe mucho agua o líquidos sin calorías. Lo más importante es, comas lo que comas, tomarlo con moderación. Si tienes alguna duda, habla con un médico o un nutricionista profesional.*

Mark Scheme:

0-8	- Award one mark for each correct letter, for a maximum of eight. - Multiple, incorrect, or illegible answers in a single box do not gain a mark for that question.

Informes

5 (a)	**Place** – *Bank*	[1]
(b)	**Event** – *(Teachers') Strike*	[1]
	Place – *School*	[1]
(c)	**Event** – *Car crash/Traffic accident*	[1]
	Place – *Motorway*	[1]
(d)	**Event** – *Earthquake*	[1]
	Place – *New York/East Coast of USA*	[1]

For this exercise, you need to be alert to pick out specific information from a news bulletin. This tests both your core vocabulary and your general comprehension skills.

Sometimes both sets of key information (**what** and **where**) will occur very close to each other and you will need to make a note, or write your answer in shorthand, and then come back to it during a pause – see *TOP TIP: Make shorthand notes* in **Listening Paper 1, Question 7(a)**.

This is the case in **(a)** where we are told about a *robo en el banco central*, although the **event** answer is given as the example. As you can see from the example, one- or two-word answers are expected, so don't write much more than this. Writing down everything you hear may indicate to the examiner that you haven't understood the task, or that you haven't been able to extract the most specific, relevant information.

In **(b)** there is a strike by the teachers at a public school – if you missed the relevant words *huelga* and *colegio*, there is a further clue in that the *profesores* have *demandas* for *igualdad de pago*. In **(c)** there has been an accident on the motorway, and **(d)** mentions an earthquake that has affected New York City and much of the east coast of the USA, either of which is acceptable as the answer to **Place**.

(a) M: *Ayer la policía llegó a la escena de un **robo** en el **banco** central. La policía está buscando a los ladrones y ruega que cualquiera que tenga información se presente.*

(b) F: *A partir de hoy, los profesores de **un colegio** público están en **huelga**. ¿Sus demandas? Igualdad de pago para sus compañeras femeninas.*

(c) M: *Se advierte que, debido a un gran **accidente de tráfico** en la **autopista**, habrá muchos retrasos hasta que lleguen las autoridades.*

(d) F: *Hay muchas personas heridas en la ciudad de **Nueva York** hoy, después de que **un terremoto** destrozó mucha parte **de la costa este de los Estados Unidos**.*

Mark Scheme:

0-7	- Award one mark for each correct answer – seven in total. - No mark for copying down entire sentences or non-specific answers, indicating guesswork.

El mundo del trabajo

6 (a)	**Positivo** – *Es fascinante/Cada día es diferente*	[1]
(b)	**Positivo** – *Puedes elegir los días de trabajo*	[1]
	Negativo – *(No le gustan/No le caen bien) sus colegas/ sus colegas son groseros/hay acoso*	[1]
(c)	**Positivo** – *Más sueldo/dinero/Le han subido el sueldo* OR: *Puede ir de vacaciones pronto <u>porque le han subido el sueldo</u>*	[1]
	Negativo – *Demasiada responsabilidad/Cuentan demasiado con ella/Se siente bajo presión*	[1]

The technique for this question is very similar to **Question 5**: apply your knowledge of vocabulary and your comprehension skills to extract the relevant information from the recording. Again, as you can see from the example, you only need one or two words or a short phrase to convey the answer. Therefore, be wary of writing too much and focus on sticking to the task within the time. Either carefully quoting from the recording (one or two words) or an accurate and precise paraphrase (in Spanish) would gain you the marks.

You're looking out for positive or negative adjectives, qualifying adverbs such as *muy, mucho, tan* or *demasiado*, and superlatives, all of which suggest opinions. Also look out for words that **introduce opinions**, as well as words that indicate a **change**

in opinion, such as *pero, sin embargo, no obstante* etc. Compare this to *TOP TIP: Look for opinions* in **Listening Paper 1, Question 8**.

In **(a)**, the speaker immediately tells us that she loves (*me encanta*) her job and gives the reasons that every day is different and the work is fascinating (*me fascina*). Either of those two reasons is an acceptable positive aspect. The negative here (the example) is introduced with *sin embargo*. The order won't always necessarily be a positive followed by a negative; it could be the other way around.

The speaker in **(b)** starts by saying that going to work every morning is a challenge (*desafío*) and backs that up with his negative reason: that he doesn't get on with his colleagues. He expands on this, saying that they are rude and there is bullying. Any of these reasons would be correct, or you could simply write *sus colegas* as the negative aspect to his job. He does, however, say that being able to choose the days he works is *la única salvación*.

The speaker in **(c)** also begins with a negative: that she has a lot of responsibility. In another context, this could be given as a positive, but it is made clear that she regards it as a negative aspect of her job with *me molesta* and her reason: that she feels under pressure. Her positive aspect is introduced by the phrase *menos mal* (= luckily): they have increased her wage. The fact that she will soon be able to go on holiday is not in itself sufficient as a positive aspect of her job – you must convey the idea that she will be able to go on holiday <u>because of</u> her increased pay.

Full Transcript
(a) F: *A mí me encanta mi trabajo. Cada día es diferente y el trabajo me fascina. Sin embargo, las horas son muy largas. Tengo que levantarme a las seis y regreso a casa a las nueve o diez de la noche.*
(b) M: *Es un desafío ir a trabajar cada mañana. No me caen bien mis colegas – son groseros y hay mucho acoso. La única salvación es que puedo elegir los días en los que trabajo.*
(c) F: *Me molesta que ahora tenga demasiada responsabilidad. Ahora hay un equipo muy joven que cuenta conmigo y siempre me siento bajo presión. ¡Menos mal que me han subido el sueldo porque pronto me permitirá irme de vacaciones!*

Mark Scheme:

0-5	- Award one mark for each correct answer – five in total. - No mark for copying down entire sentences or non-specific answers, indicating guesswork.

Bolsas de plástico

---

7 (a) When does this change come into effect?

From the end of this month [1]

This section requires you to answer in English, although full sentences in **listening papers** aren't necessary (unless otherwise stated in the instructions) as there often isn't time. You will have to be precise and accurate in your translation of the recording, however – see *TOP TIP: Be specific* in **Listening Paper 1, Question 9(a)**.

For example, we are told that the new measures will come into place <u>from the end of this month</u>. Therefore, simply writing "this month" is not specific enough to gain a mark. "From the beginning of next month" *might* get the mark, but is risky and therefore best avoided.

… no va a vender las bolsas de plástico de uso individual. ***A partir del fin de este mes****, los clientes del supermercado …*

Mark scheme:

0/1	- Information is not supplied or not relevant. - Vague or incorrect/mistranslated answers do not score.
1/1	- Candidate has identified and supplied the correct answer.

---

7 (b) What are the two new options?

Bring your own bags [1]
Buy a reusable bag [1]

The necessary information occurs immediately after question **7(a)**, specifically using the phrase *dos opciones* to signal the relevance to **7(b)**. The recording also uses the construction *o … o* (either … or) to introduce two distinct reasons. There is very little room for imaginative interpretations of the information, so be specific with your translations.

---

*… los clientes del supermercado tendrán <u>dos opciones</u>: puedes, <u>o</u> **traer tus propias bolsas** contigo cuando vas de compras, <u>o</u> **comprar una bolsa reutilizable**, la llamada "bolsa para la vida".*

Mark Scheme:

0/2	- Information is not supplied or not relevant.
1/2	- Candidate has identified and supplied **one** option that shoppers can do.
2/2	- Candidate has identified and supplied **two** separate options that the shoppers can do.

---

7 (c) What happens if your bag is damaged?

The shop will replace it (free of charge) 　　　　　[1]

Again, a direct translation of the recording would be a perfect answer – the shop will replace damaged bags. The extra information, that this is a free service, is not necessary to gain the mark.

---

*Si tu bolsa reutilizable es <u>dañada</u>, la tienda **la reemplazará** sin cargo.*

Mark scheme:

0/1	- Information is not supplied or not relevant. - Vague or incorrect/mistranslated answers do not score.
1/1	- Candidate has identified and supplied the correct answer: that the shop will replace damaged bags for life. - The fact that this service is free of charge is not necessary to gaining a mark, but is not sufficient on its own.

---

7 (d) What effect does the supermarket think this change will have? Give two ideas.

Any TWO of:
Reduce the sale of plastic bags
Less litter (on the streets)
Fewer bags going to landfills
Fewer bags ending up in the oceans or seas 　　　　　[2]

The recording gives a lot of information at once, almost any part of which would be one correct answer, so taking shorthand notes and filling in the gaps during the pauses would be a wise approach. The mark scheme requires two <u>separate</u> points, so saying that fewer bags will end up in the oceans and seas is <u>one</u> point, not two. However, landfills and oceans are classed as separate ideas.

> *<u>Según el supermercado</u>, debido a este cambio, **el número de bolsas de plástico** que se venden **disminuirá**, lo que significa **una reducción de basura** en las calles y **menos bolsas** que terminan **en vertederos** o **en los océanos y mares**.*

Mark Scheme:

0/2	- Information is not supplied or not relevant.
1/2	- Candidate has identified and supplied **one** effect that this change will have.
2/2	- Candidate has identified and supplied **two** <u>separate</u> effects that this change will have.

---

7 (e) Who is this good news for, according to the government?

> *The environment*
> OR:
> *Marine life* [1]

Following on from the previous sentence in which we were told that fewer bags will end up in landfills and in the oceans and seas, the government official says that while (*mientras*) the initiative may be a little inconvenient for shoppers, it represents good news in the long term (*a largo plazo*) for the environment, especially marine life. Either of these will gain the mark for this question.

> *La ministra de medio ambiente ha elogiado esta iniciativa, y dice que mientras esta noticia puede ser un poco inconveniente para los consumidores, a largo plazo representa <u>buenas noticias</u> **para el medio ambiente**, sobre todo para **la vida marina**.*

Mark scheme:

0/1	- Information is not supplied or not relevant. - Vague or incorrect/mistranslated answers do not score.
1/1	- Candidate has identified and supplied the correct answer: that the move will benefit the <u>environment</u>. - "Marine life" is also accepted as an answer.

7 (f) Who does this news not affect?

Online shoppers [1]

The relevant information for this question is introduced with *no obstante* and we are told that for people who buy online (*en línea* – very standard GCSE vocabulary), things are as before (*como antes*). They <u>can</u> opt for a bagless delivery, although this information isn't relevant to answering this question.

<u>No obstante</u>, para los millones de **clientes que compran en línea**, las cosas son <u>como</u> <u>antes</u>, aunque se puede optar por una entrega sin bolsas.

Mark scheme:

0/1	- Information is not supplied or not relevant. - Vague or incorrect/mistranslated answers do not score.
1/1	- Candidate has identified and supplied the correct answer: that online shoppers will be unaffected by this.

7 (g) What does the supermarket now hope will happen?

Other supermarkets will do the same/follow their example [1]

The information for this question comes as a direct quote from a spokesperson for the company. You can answer with either a literal translation, or a succinct paraphrase. She hopes that, as the company has taken the first step to fulfilling their obligation to protecting the environment, other chains (*cadenas*) will follow their example and do the same.

Según <u>un portavoz de la empresa</u>, este paso es el primer paso para cumplir la obligación de todos <u>a proteger el medio ambiente</u>: "Ahora es tiempo para que <u>las otras cadenas</u> **sigan nuestro ejemplo y hagan lo mismo**. <u>Espero que lo hagan.</u>"

Mark scheme:

0/1	- Information is not supplied or not relevant. - Vague or incorrect/mistranslated answers do not score.
1/1	- Candidate has identified and supplied the correct answer: that other chains of supermarkets will follow the example and do the same. Either half of this sentence, or both, is accepted.

Full Transcript

M: *Una de las cadenas más grandes de supermercados en Gran Bretaña ha anunciado que ya no va a vender las bolsas de plástico de uso individual. A partir del fin de este mes, los clientes del supermercado tendrán dos opciones: traer tus propias bolsas contigo cuando vas de compras o comprar una bolsa reutilizable, la llamada "bolsa para la vida". Estas nuevas bolsas están hechas de plástico reciclado y costarán 10 peniques, o sea unos 13 céntimos. Si tu bolsa reutilizable es dañada, la tienda la reemplazará sin cargo.*

Según el supermercado, debido a este cambio, el número de bolsas de plástico que se venden disminuirá, lo que significa una reducción en la basura en las calles y menos bolsas que terminan en vertederos o en los océanos y mares. La ministra de medio ambiente ha elogiado esta iniciativa, y dice que mientras esta noticia puede ser un poco inconveniente para los consumidores, a largo plazo representa buenas noticias para el medio ambiente, sobre todo para la vida marina.

No obstante, para los millones de clientes que compran en línea, las cosas son como antes, aunque se puede optar por una entrega sin bolsas. Según un portavoz de la empresa, éste es el primer paso para cumplir la obligación de todos a proteger el medio ambiente:
F: *"Ahora es tiempo para que las otras cadenas sigan nuestro ejemplo y hagan lo mismo. Espero que lo hagan."*

Entrevista a un escritor

8 (a) ¿De qué género es su nuevo libro?	
Ciencia ficción	[1]

In this section, you have to listen to an interview and glean the relevant information from the writer's responses. You have to answer in Spanish – although not in full sentences – but you can make notes throughout in any language – see *TOP TIP: Make shorthand notes* in **Listening Paper 1, Question 7(a).**

Question **(a)** has a common trap at the heart of it: although he mentions his romance novels, and makes references to love and passion, the writer begins by saying that his <u>new</u> work is different, and has more in common with science fiction. He goes on to say that it is set in a parallel universe (another hint that it is a science fiction novel) where love doesn't exist (therefore not a romantic novel).

> *Bueno, es algo <u>diferente</u>. Hasta ahora he escrito muchas novelas de amor, con mucha pasión y con el ideal del amor romántico. Esta obra tiene elementos románticos, claro, pero <u>tiene</u> <u>más cosas en común</u> con la* **ciencia ficción**. *Está ambientada en un universo paralelo donde el amor no existe.*

Mark scheme:

0/1	- Information is not supplied or not relevant. - Answers **not** in Spanish throughout the section will score **zero** marks.
1/1	- Candidate has identified and supplied the correct answer: that the writer's new book will be science fiction.

---

8 (b) ¿Qué le inspira escribir? Da dos ideas.

Any TWO of:
Lo que ocurre en el mundo
Las noticias
La situación política/social del mundo
Las personas (comunes)
Celebridades
Sus amigos/su familia   [2]

Just like question **7(d)**, the recording gives a lot of information at once, and you are required to identify two separate things that inspire the writer. He gives some very general answers, such as 'what is happening in the world', and people that he meets on whom he bases new characters. He also gets specific, referring to the global political and social situation and to people such as celebrities, and his own friends and family.

TOP TIP: Keep your points distinct.

Any of these ideas or groups of people are enough to score one mark each (for a maximum of two), but be careful that your two points are distinct enough to count as separate ideas. 'The global social and political situation' would only count as one idea, and therefore only score <u>one</u> mark. 'Friends and family' would also only score one mark. 'Celebrities' and 'the common man' count as two separate ideas and would score full marks. However, writing that 'he is inspired by people such as the common man' would only gain one mark.

Therefore, to be certain of getting full marks, try to make your two points as clear and distinct as you can. For example: *lo que ocurre en el mundo* and *las personas que ha conocido*.

---

*Me inspiro en **lo que ocurre en el mundo**, leo **las noticias** cada día y encuentro nuevas ideas de **la situación política y social del mundo**. También me fascinan las personas, y mis personajes son una mezcla de **las** personas que he conocido en mi vida, tanto **celebridades** como **personas comunes**, **mis amigos**, **mi familia**…*

Mark Scheme:

0/2	- Information is not supplied or not relevant.
1/2	- Candidate has identified and supplied **one** thing that inspires the writer.
2/2	- Candidate has identified and supplied **two** separate things that inspire the writer.

---

8 (c) Según él, ¿qué responsabilidad tiene un escritor?

Interesarse en todo
OR:
Escribir con verdad (emocional)   [1]

The writer goes on to say that he thinks he feels he has *la obligación* (= *responsabilidad*) to be interested in everything, and to tell his story with as much truth as possible. Either of these ideas would gain you the mark. He also explains that he means <u>emotional</u> truth, rather than facts.

---

*Como autor tengo la obligación de **interesarme por todo**. Luego, tengo que **contar mi historia con tanta verdad como sea posible**. Quiero decir, no se deben recitar hechos históricos, sino que lo importante es contar una verdad emocional. …*

Mark scheme:

0/1	- Information is not supplied or not relevant. - Answers **not** in Spanish throughout the section will score **zero** marks.
1/1	- Candidate has identified and supplied the correct answer: that he feels writers have an obligation to be interested in everything OR to tell their story with as much (emotional) truth as possible.

8 (d) ¿Qué consejo tiene para escritores jóvenes? Menciona dos ideas.
Any TWO of: *Interesarse en todo/todo es relevante/interesante* *Leer todo el tiempo* *Aprender nuevos estilos y técnicas (al leer)* *Escribir/practicar cuando sea posible* *No asustarse por cometer errores*   [2]

This final question is another opportunity to score two marks by isolating two specific, separate points from a fairly long passage of dialogue. He repeats his earlier point that a writer should be interested in everything – although it might be safer to make a different point if you have already used this information in **8(c)**.

With this in mind, the advice that *todo es relevante* would count as an explanation for *interesarse en todo*, not as a separate point. Likewise, *leer todo el tiempo* is a distinct piece of advice but *aprender nuevos estilos y técnicas* is a byproduct of the previous idea. Either would score a mark, but you wouldn't get two marks for writing both. *Practicar* and *escribir siempre que sea posible* are also the same point. His final advice is not to be afraid of making mistakes, which is a new idea.

> *Como dije:* **interesarse en todo**. *Todo es interesante, todo es relevante. También,* **leer todo el tiempo** *y aprender nuevos estilos y técnicas. Finalmente,* **escribe siempre** *que sea posible. No importa el contenido, con tal de que estés* **practicando**. **No te asustes por cometer errores**.

Mark Scheme:

0/2	- Information is not supplied or not relevant.
1/2	- Candidate has identified and supplied **one** piece of advice for young writers.
2/2	- Candidate has identified and supplied **two** separate pieces of advice for young writers.

Full transcript

F: *¿De qué trata tu próximo libro?*

M: *Bueno, es algo diferente. Hasta ahora, he escrito muchas novelas de amor, con mucha pasión y con el ideal del amor romántico. Esta obra tiene elementos románticos, claro, pero tiene más cosas en común con la ciencia ficción. Está ambientado en un universo paralelo donde el amor no existe.*

F: *Y, ¿por qué has decidido publicar una obra así?*

M: *Me inspiro en lo que ocurre en el mundo, leo las noticias cada día y encuentro nuevas ideas de la situación política y social del mundo. También me fascinan las personas, y mis personajes son una mezcla de las personas que he conocido en mi vida, tanto celebridades como personas comunes, mis amigos, mi familia… Como autor tengo la obligación de interesarme por todo. Luego, tengo que contar mi historia con tanta verdad como sea posible. Quiero decir, no se deben recitar hechos históricos, sino lo importante es contar una verdad emocional. Y ahora mismo, yo creo que el mundo necesita una historia así.*

F: *Genial. Y finalmente, ¿qué recomendarías a los jóvenes que quieren ser escritores?*

M: *Como dije: interesarse en todo. Todo es interesante, todo es relevante. También, leer todo el tiempo y aprender nuevos estilos y técnicas. Finalmente, escribe siempre que sea posible. No importa el contenido, con tal de que estés practicando. No te asustes por cometer errores.*

END OF SOLUTIONS FOR PAPER 2

Listening Paper 3

> *Visit **www.rsleducational.co.uk/spanishaudio** to download the audio file for this paper.*

If you wish to complete this paper in timed conditions, allow 45 minutes plus 5 minutes' reading time.

Instructions

- Use **black** ink or ballpoint pen.
- Answer **all** questions.
- Answer the questions in the spaces provided.
  - *There may be more space than you require.*
- Dictionaries are **not** allowed.

Advice

- You have 5 minutes to read through the paper before the recording starts.
- You will hear each extract twice. You may write at any time during the examination. There will be a pause between each question.
- Read each question **carefully** before attempting it.
- The marks available for each question are given in [square brackets]. These give you an indication of how long to spend on each question.
- There is a total of **50 marks** available for this paper.
- Leave time to check your answers at the end, if possible.

Answer ALL questions.

Salamanca

1   Julieta habla sobre su región. ¿Qué **cuatro** cosas menciona? Pon una equis [X] en cada casilla correcta.

Julieta is talking about her region. Which **four** things does she mention? Put a cross [X] in each correct box.

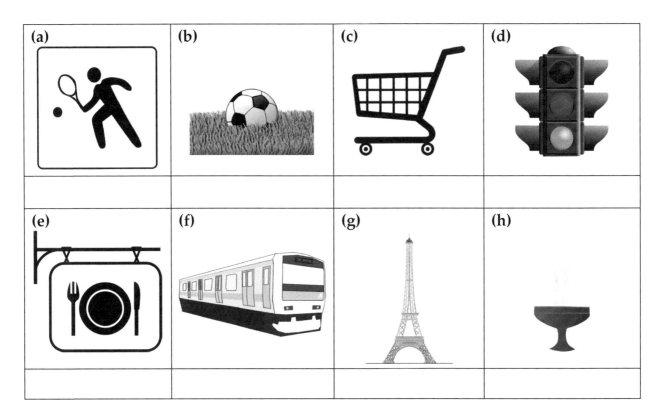

(Total for Question 1 = 4 marks)

En el aeropuerto

2   Llegas al aeropuerto para volar a Barcelona. Escucha la grabación y pon una
    equis **[X]** en cada casilla correcta.

    You arrive at the airport to fly to Barcelona. Listen to the recording and put a
    cross **[X]** in each correct box.

(a) What gate number is the flight to Barcelona?

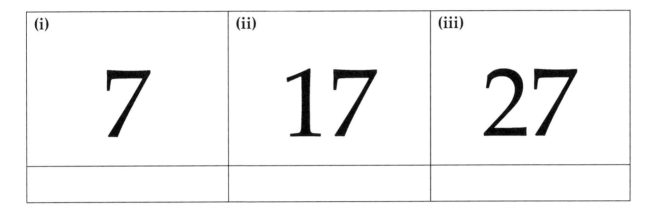

(i)	(ii)	(iii)
7	17	27

(b) At what time is your flight?

(i)	(ii)	(iii)
6:45	7:15	1:30

(c) How long will the flight last?

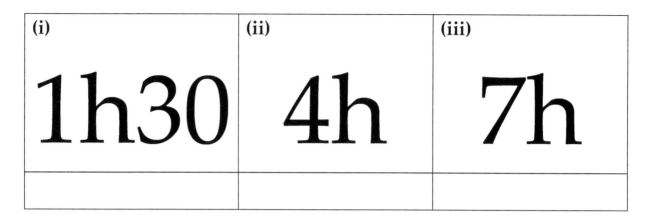

(i)	(ii)	(iii)
1h30	4h	7h

(d) What is the weather **currently** like in Barcelona?

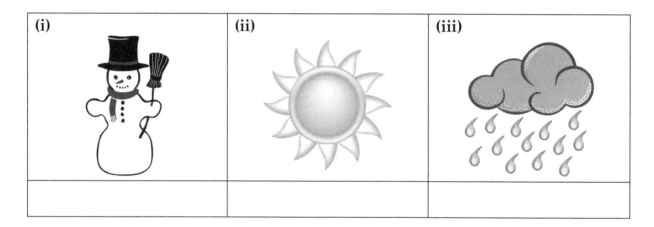

(i)	(ii)	(iii)

(e) What can you buy in the shop?

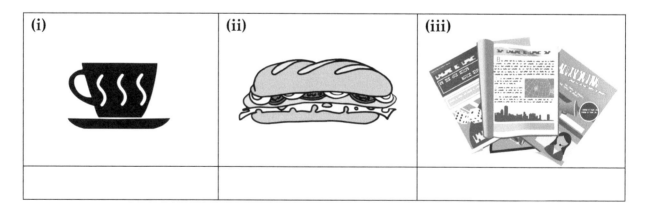

(i)	(ii)	(iii)

(Total for Question 2 = 5 marks)

Bolsa perdida

3   Tu amiga ha perdido su bolso. Escribe **en inglés cinco** cosas que contenía.

Your friend has lost her bag. Write down **in English five** things that were in it.

....

....

....

....

....

....

....

(Total for Question 3 = 5 marks)

La salud

4   ¿Qué hacen estas personas para mantenerse sanas? Pon una equis [X] en cada casilla correcta.

What do these people do to stay healthy? Put a cross [X] in each correct box.

	A	B	C	D	E	F	G	H
Ejemplo: Josefina		X						
(a) Pablo								
(b) Flor								
(c) Andrea								
(d) Jesús								
(e) Sofía								

(Total for Question 4 = 5 marks)

Mis programas favoritos

5   Bernarda habla de sus programas favoritos. ¿Qué dice? Completa las frases con las letras correctas.

Bernarda is talking about her favourite programmes. What does she say? Complete the phrases with the correct letters.

A En el cine	**B** Sola	**C** Acción
D Hacen ruido	**E** Comen	**F** Comedia
G Misterio	**H** En casa	**I** Amor

Ejemplo: Sus programas favoritos de televisión son dramas de ...	G
(a) Su género preferido de película es ...	
(b) Prefiere ver películas ...	
(c) A Bernarda no le gustan las personas que ... en el cine.	

(Total for Question 5 = 3 marks)

Transporte

6   Estas personas hablan sobre el transporte. Escucha lo que dicen y escribe **en español** los aspectos positivos y negativos de cada modo de transporte.

These people are talking about transport. Listen to what they say and write down **in Spanish** the positive and negative aspects of each mode of transport.

Ejemplo: Autocar

Positivo	Negativo
Barato	Viaje largo

(a) Tren

Positivo	Negativo

(b) Avión

Positivo	Negativo

(c) Coche

Positivo	Negativo

(Total for Question 6 = 6 marks)

Las calorías en la comida basura

7   Escucha este informe sobre comida basura y contesta las preguntas que están debajo.

Listen to this report about junk food and answer the question below.

¿Qué **seis** frases son correctas? Pon una equis **[X]** en cada casilla apropiada.
Which **six** statements are correct? Put a cross **[X]** in each correct box.

Ejemplo: Esta iniciativa está diseñada para luchar contra la obesidad de niños.	**X**
(a) Estos cambios se realizarán en menos de doce meses.	
(b) Esta noticia no afecta a los restaurantes más ricos.	
(c) Muchas empresas posiblemente tendrían que usar otros ingredientes en el futuro.	
(d) Esta iniciativa ya ha tenido mucho éxito.	
(e) Este tipo de iniciativa es la primera que el Gobierno ha intentado realizar.	
(f) Hoy en día los productos de comida basura usan menos sal.	
(g) Las restricciones en la cantidad de sal y azúcar se introdujeron hace unos diez años.	
(h) Los anuncios tienen una influencia dañina en la salud de los jóvenes.	
(i) El Gobierno es responsable de los anuncios.	
(j) Muchas compañías de comida rápida también proveen otras opciones que son mejores para la salud.	
(k) La ley requiere que todos productos alimenticios muestren la información nutricional.	

(Total for Question 7 = 6 marks)

Entrevista con Ángela González

8   Escucha esta entrevista con una deportista joven y luego contesta las
       preguntas que están debajo **en inglés**. No tienes que escribir frases completas.

       Listen to this interview with a young sportswoman, and then answer the
       questions below **in English**. You don't have to write full sentences.

(a) Why are Ángela's achievements notable?   [1]

....

....

(b) What does she put her success down to? Give **two** ideas.   [2]

....

....

(c) What are her immediate plans for the future?   [1]

....

(d) What does she feel is her greatest sporting moment?   [1]

....

(e) What are her plans for life after tennis?   [1]

....

(f) What concerns her? Give **two** ideas.   [2]

....

....

(Total for Question 8 = 8 marks)

La informática

9   Escucha esta grabación sobre las clases de informática. Luego, contesta las preguntas que están debajo **en español**. No tienes que escribir frases completas.

Listen to this recording about IT classes. Then answer the questions below **in Spanish**. You don't have to write full sentences.

(a) ¿Cuál es la estadística que preocupa a los expertos en informática?   [1]

....

(b) ¿Cómo es la situación en la industria en general?   [1]

....

(c) ¿Cuáles son las **dos** cosas que creen los expertos?   [2]

....

....

(d) ¿Por qué no hay sólo malas noticias?   [1]

....

....

(e) Da **dos** razones por las que las chicas no quieren estudiar informática en el colegio.   [2]

....

....

(f) Según la señora López, ¿qué se necesita cambiar? Da **una** idea. [1]

…………… *the exclusive use of the purchaser – Not to be copied – © RSL Educational Ltd* …………

(Total for Question 9 = 8 marks)

TOTAL FOR PAPER = 50 MARKS

Blank Page

Listening Paper 3 – SOLUTIONS

Salamanca

---

1 Julieta habla sobre su región. ¿Qué cuatro cosas menciona?

> *(b) (c) (e) (f)*   [4]

The information in the question, as well as the title (Salamanca is the name of a city in Spain), gives you an idea as to what area of your core vocabulary is being tested: city and local area.

Use the pause before the recording to think of the words which correspond to the pictures, as well as synonyms that you might hear – see *TOP TIP: Use your time wisely* in **Listening Paper 1**, **Question 6**. For example, the food sign in **(e)** could be *un restaurante, un café*, or just *comida*. In this case, Julieta refers to both restaurants and bars. The shopping trolley icon in **(c)** might refer to *un supermercado, un centro comercial*, or perhaps *ir de compras* in general. In this case, she mentions the large shopping centre as a place to buy clothes – understanding either of these pieces of information would lead you to the correct answer. She then says that she goes to the stadium in Madrid to watch the football, and that she goes by train.

There are **four** marks available: one per correct answer. Double-check that you have exactly four boxes crossed – no more, no fewer. Not all pictures will be used and the answers won't necessarily occur in the same order as the pictures.

Full Transcript – the answers are given in **bold**

*F: Vivo en la ciudad de Salamanca. Me encanta porque hay muchos **restaurantes** y bares en la plaza mayor, además **de un gran centro comercial** donde puedo comprar ropa. Además, estamos bastante cerca de Madrid, y cada semana voy con mi padre al estadio para ver el **fútbol**. Sólo se tarda una hora y media en **tren**.*

Mark Scheme:

0-4	- Award one mark for each correct answer, up to four. - Deduct one mark for each incorrect answer, even if the correct answers are also crossed. - *Therefore, crossing eight boxes would mean four wrong answers and score 0 marks.*

En el aeropuerto

---

2 (a) What number terminal do you need for the flight to Barcelona?

    (ii)   [1]

This section tests your ability to listen carefully and pinpoint the key information from your knowledge of core vocabulary.

Once you have completed this section, **check your answers**. Make sure you have answered each question, and that you don't have multiple answers for a single question. If you have, erase or put a neat line through the wrong answer (✗), to signal to the examiner that you have changed your mind.

The key information (*número diecisiete*) for question **2(a)** occurs in the middle of the sentence.

---

2 (b) At what time is your flight?

    (i)   [1]

---

2 (c) How long will the flight last?

    (i)   [1]

The key information for both questions **2(b)** and **(c)** occurs close together and requires you to know how to tell the time: *siete **menos** cuarto* is quarter **to** seven (not quarter past). The speaker then also says that the flight will last an hour and a half. You need to understand these two pieces of information are separate, and not be confused into thinking that the flight leaves at 1:30 or that it will last 7 hours, for example – see *TOP TIP: Pay attention to the whole sentence* in **Listening Paper 1, Question 2**.

---

2 (d) What is the weather currently like in Barcelona?

    (iii)   [1]

The trick in question **(d)** is finding what the weather is **currently** like in Barcelona (*está lloviendo*), not what they hope it will be when you land (*hacer sol*) even though it is winter (*invierno*). The key word is highlighted in the question and introduced in the recording with *actualmente* (a false friend meaning 'currently', not 'actually').

---

2 (e) What can you buy in the shop?

(iii) [1]

Finally, as there is still a wait to board the flight, you are told that you can buy something to read. Food is served on the plane itself. Therefore, picture *(iii)* is the only corresponding icon.

Full transcript

M: *Bienvenidos a la puerta de embarque número **diecisiete** con destino a Barcelona. Para el vuelo hacia Málaga, por favor diríjanse a la puerta número veinte. Este vuelo saldrá a **las siete menos cuarto** y llegaremos al Aeropuerto de Barcelona en **una hora y media**. Actualmente **está lloviendo** en Barcelona y hace mucho frío pero esperamos que haga sol cuando aterricemos, aunque sea invierno. Todavía nos quedan dos horas pero pueden visitar la tienda donde pueden comprar **algo para leer** durante el viaje. Se sirve comida en el avión. Gracias por volar con nosotros.*

Mark Scheme:

0-5	- Award one mark for each correct answer. - Multiple answers or unanswered questions score **zero** marks for that question.

Bolsa Perdida

3 Tu amiga ha perdido su bolso. Escribe en inglés cinco cosas que contenía.	
Books	[1]
Her diary	[1]
Pen	[1]
Pencils	[1]
Rubber/eraser	[1]
Computer	[1]
Wallet/Purse	[1]
Credit cards	[1]
	[maximum 5]

For this question, you are required to pick out the words that indicate the items in your friend's bag, and translate them into English accurately. There are **five** possible marks, but more than five things are mentioned in the recording. Writing fewer than five will of course mean you don't score full marks, but if you know more than five, you may write them down too, to be sure of getting maximum marks.

You can make notes at any time, including during the recordings. However, as much of the essential information occurs very close together, just make quick shorthand notes and write the answers properly during a pause – see **TOP TIP: Make shorthand notes** in **Listening Paper 1**, **Question 7(a)**.

One trap that you should watch out for: she lost her mobile phone **last** week, which is how she knew to check if it had been handed in, but it is not mentioned as being one of the missing items in the bag. Her purse and her credit cards count as **two** separate items, even though the cards are inside the purse.

Full transcript

F: *¿Has visto mi bolso? Estoy muy preocupada. Contiene todos **mis libros** para mis próximas clases, incluso **mi diario**. También **mi boli, mis lápices** y **una goma de borrar**. ¿Qué debo hacer? Cuando perdí mi teléfono móvil la semana pasada alguien lo entregó a la recepción, pero ya he ido y mi bolso no está. Lo único caro que contenía es **mi ordenador**, aunque **mi cartera, con mis tarjetas de crédito,** también está dentro.*

Mark Scheme:

0-5	- Award one mark for each correct answer.
	- Incorrect answers do not score, but do not lose a mark either.

La salud

4 ¿Qué hacen estas personas para mantenerse sanas?	
(a) *Pablo – C*	[1]
(b) *Flor – A*	[1]
(c) *Andrea – G*	[1]
(d) *Jesús – D*	[1]
(e) *Sofía – F*	[1]

This question about health and sport requires you to understand the meaning of the individual sentences and cross the most appropriate box.

```
┌─────────────────────────────────────────────────────────────────────┐
│                    TOP TIP: Listen in chunks.                         │
│                                                                       │
│  It's often the case when learning languages that we try and          │
│  understand every individual word; but a much better, more natural    │
│  approach is to think in chunks. Therefore, listen to the whole       │
│  sentence and listen out for clues and words you do understand, but   │
│  don't get frustrated or preoccupied by the ones you can't. After a   │
│  while you'll be able to focus on the meaning of the whole idea,      │
│  rather than the individual words.                                    │
└─────────────────────────────────────────────────────────────────────┘
```

In the example sentence, the answer is given explicitly (*correr*) but she also tells us that she's going to participate in the marathon, which is a further clue as to the sport. Likewise, Pablo in **(a)** explicitly says that his favourite sport is *la equitación* and then backs this up with *montar a caballo*. Flor **(b)** mentions *fruta* as well as the advice to eat five portions a day.

Andrea's answer in **(c)** is a little more hidden, as she mentions her local gym and the fact that it has an exercise room, but she uses this room to practice dancing (*bailar*). Be sure to listen to the entire sentence, and not rush to conclusions on merely hearing the words *gimnasio* or *ejercicio*. Similarly, Jesús **(d)** also mentions that he goes to the gym, but in order to swim (*hacer natación*) rather than lift weights. Finally, Sofía in **(e)** gives the answer explicitly (*llevar una botella de agua*) but has already given the clue that it is easy to dehydrate (*deshidratarse*) when doing exercise.

Full transcript

Ejemplo: F: *A mí me encanta **correr**. El mes que viene voy a participar en <u>la maratón</u>.*

(a) M: *Mi deporte favorito es **la equitación**. Me flipa <u>montar a caballo</u> y me mantiene en buena forma.*

(b) F: *Para mí es imprescindible comer mucha **fruta**, o sea, por lo menos <u>cinco porciones al día</u>.*

(c) F: *Mi gimnasio local tiene una <u>sala de ejercicios</u> con <u>espejos</u> en las paredes donde puedo **bailar** en paz.*

(d) M: *Yo voy al gimnasio tres veces a la semana para hacer **natación**.*

(e) F: *Yo sé que es muy fácil <u>deshidratarse</u> cuando haces ejercicio. Por eso siempre llevo una **botella de agua** conmigo.*

Mark Scheme:

0-5	- Award one mark for each correct answer. - Multiple answers or unanswered questions score **zero** marks for that question.

Mis programas favoritos

5 (a) F *Comedia*	[1]
(b) A *En el cine*	[1]
(c) D *Hacen ruido*	[1]

Make sure you have listened to and understood the whole recording. With multiple-choice questions such as these it is often possible to eliminate the majority of the options for each question before you have even heard the recording, according to whether you are looking for an adjective, a noun, or a verb – see *TOP TIP: Find the possible answers first* in **Listening Paper 1**, **Question 5**.

Both the example and question **(a)** require very similar answers, specifically a type of film or TV genre. As *G Misterio* is already given as the answer in the example, this narrows the choice for **(a)** down to *C Acción*, *F Comedia*, or possibly *I Amor*. The recording doesn't explicitly mention the genre, but Bernarda does say that she likes to laugh and watch something funny, so the correct answer is *F Comedia*.

Question **5(b)** is a little more ambiguous, and possible answers include *A En el cine* or its opposite *H En casa*, or even *B Sola*. However, within the same sentence we are told that she thinks it is better (the same idea as *preferir*) to go to the cinema with friends, so the answer is *A*. She does mention staying *en casa*, but only to compare the atmosphere unfavourably to the cinema.

Question **5(c)** is more straightforward, and we are looking for a verb in the 3rd person plural and in the present tense (to agree with *las personas que …*). The speaker says that what she finds most irritating is when people talk during the film, so *D Hacen ruido* is a much better fit than *E Comen*.

Full transcript
F: *Cuando descanso en casa me encanta ver la tele, sobre todo los dramas de* **misterio** *porque me encantan las tramas. Sin embargo, cuando veo películas* <u>me gusta reír</u> *y* **ver algo gracioso**. *Para mí es* **mejor ir al cine** *con mis amigas porque cuando te quedas en casa* <u>no hay el mismo ambiente</u>. *También puedes llevar tu propia comida, porque así es más barato. No obstante, ¡lo que* <u>más me molesta</u> *es cuando la gente enfrente de nosotros* **habla** *durante toda la película!*

Mark Scheme:

0-5	- Award one mark for each correct answer. - Multiple answers or unanswered questions score **zero** marks for that question.

Transporte Público

6 (a) *Tren*

      Positivo – *(Más) rápido* [1]

      Negativo – *Incómodo/no puede relajarse* [1]

(b) *Avión*

      Positivo –   *Cómodo/comodidad*

      OR: *Lujoso/lujo* [1]

      Negativo –   *Caro/cuesta demasiado (dinero)* [1]

(c) *Coche*

      Positivo – *Conveniente* [1]

      Negativo – *Estresante/agotador*

      OR: *Se tiene que estar alerta* [1]

For this question, you need only one or two words, or a succinct phrase **in Spanish** to convey each answer. You need to be selective and work within the timespan, so either quote carefully (one or two words), or accurately and precisely paraphrase what you hear – see *TOP TIP: Be specific* in **Listening Paper 1, Question 9(a)**.

TOP TIP: Find positive/negative opinions.

There are many ways in which positive or negative opinions can be introduced in listening and reading questions – compare this tip to *TOP TIP: Looking for opinions* in **Listening Paper 1, Question 8**. In this question, you have to determine whether the opinion is a positive or a negative one; one way is simply by identifying the adjectives. Also look out for **qualifying adverbs** such as *muy, mucho, tan* or *demasiado*, which could be used either in a positive or negative way (although *demasiado* is nearly always a bad thing!). You may also see **absolute** adverbs used, such as *siempre, jamás/nunca* or *nada* to express a strong opinion, or even **superlative** adjectives/adverbs, such as *lo mejor/peor* or *carísimo*. Finally, be on the lookout for phrases that **introduce** opinions, such as *en mi opinión, según yo, a mi parecer, pienso/creo/opino que* and *me gusta/encanta/molesta*, as well as words or phrases that indicate a **change** in opinion: *pero, sin embargo, no obstante* etc.

In this case, you are hearing a discussion – or argument – involving several forms of transport and their relative merits and drawbacks. Finding the positives and negatives here is relatively straightforward, and these can often be written using a common adjective, and if necessary with a little extra explanation. The positive and negative aspects of *un autocar* are both given as examples, to get you used to the rhythm and style of the exercise.

After that, the male voice in **(a)** suggests that a train would be quicker (than the coach in the example). You can use either the comparative (*más rapido*) or the adjective by itself. The female voice then introduces the counter-argument, that this mode of transport is uncomfortable, and explains that she would not be able to relax. Either piece of information would score you the mark – remember to **be specific**!

Question **(b)** follows a similar format. We are told that the plane offers luxury and comfort, but that it's very expensive. *Costar un ojo de la cara* is a very Spanish idiom, the equivalent of "to cost an arm and a leg", but literally translating as "an eye of the face" (as well as meaning face, *cara* also means expensive, so it's a pun)! The female speaker adds that she doesn't have the money for that, so even if you didn't grasp the idiom, understanding that she doesn't have enough money would still give you the correct answer.

Finally, in question **(c)** the male speaker gives both positive and negative opinions about the car, conceding that it would be convenient, but that it would be exhausting and stressful (either or both of these adjectives would score a mark) because one has to be alert all the time (this explanation by itself would also gain the mark).

Full transcript
Ejemplo: M: *Oye Elena. La semana que viene vamos de vacaciones. ¿Quieres ir en autocar? Será muy **barato**.*
F: *Barato, sí, pero **tarda demasiado**. El viaje <u>durará todo el día</u>.*
(a) M: *¿En tren, entonces? Es mucho más **rápido**.*
F: *Claro… pero es muy **incómodo**. No podré <u>relajarme</u>.*
(b) M: *Bueno, si quieres **lujo y comodidad**, ¿por qué no vamos en avión?*
F: *Estás bromeando, ¡**cuesta** un ojo de la cara volar! No me alcanza el <u>dinero</u> para eso. Debemos ir en coche.*
(c) M: *Es verdad que sería muy **conveniente** ir en coche. Pero si vas a conducir, es muy **estresante y agotador** porque se tiene que <u>estar alerta</u>.*
F: *Entonces, ¿por qué no cogemos el autocar?*
M: *¡Eso es lo que dije yo!*

Mark Scheme:

0-6	- Award one mark for each correct answer – six in total. - Candidate may quote succinctly from the text, or use their own words. - Vague answers may indicate guesswork and do not score. - Overly long answers do not score, as they indicate that the candidate hasn't fully understood the point.

Las calorías en la comida basura

7 ¿Qué seis frases son correctas?   *(a) (c) (f) (g) (h) (j)*   [6]

With a longer recording such as this, it is important that you read the sentences underneath first. After you have crossed the answers, be sure to check that you have exactly six answers crossed: you gain one mark for each correct cross.

Remember that you have five minutes before the recording to look at these questions. Use this time to <u>underline</u> the key words in each sentence. Make notes or simply think of synonyms or other ways the recording could paraphrase them to convey the same meaning – see *TOP TIP: Use your time wisely* in **Listening Paper 1, Question 6**. You can then review and correct your notes in the pauses - there won't be enough time to do this while the recording is playing.

In the example, we are told that the initiative is designed to combat *la obesidad de niños* (= *la obesidad infantil*).

(a) *Estos cambios se realizarán en menos de doce meses.* – TRUE
(b) *Esta noticia no afecta a los restaurantes más ricos.* – FALSE (no cross needed)
(c) *Muchas empresas posiblemente tendrían que usar otros ingredientes en el futuro.* – TRUE

We are told in the recording that the quantity of calories in fast food will be reduced within a year, which is the direct equivalent of *en menos de doce meses*. The changes will affect all supermarkets and fast food restaurants, not just the wealthiest, so **(b)** is a false sentence but **(c)** is true.

> *… la cantidad de calorías en la comida basura disminuirá <u>dentro de un año</u>. Estos cambios significarán que los supermercados y restaurantes de comida basura tendrán que reducir el tamaño de los productos o <u>cambiar los ingredientes</u> en la comida.*

En menos de doce meses = dentro de un año
Usar otros ingredientes = cambiar los ingredientes

(d) *Esta iniciativa ya ha tenido mucho éxito.* – FALSE
(e) *Este tipo de iniciativa es la primera que el Gobierno ha intentado realizar.* – FALSE
(f) *Hoy en día los productos de comida basura usan menos sal.* – TRUE
(g) *Las restricciones en la cantidad de sal y azúcar se introdujeron hace unos diez años.* – TRUE

The relevant information for the next **four** sentences occurs (in order) within the space of the next paragraph. Sentence **(d)** states that the initiative has already been successful (perfect tense), whereas the recording only says that the officals are sure that it will be successful (future tense). *Ser exitoso* and *tener éxito* mean the same thing, but the future tense of the recording contradicts the perfect tense of the sentence. The reason they are confident of success is because of the success that similar projects have had, which again contradicts the claim of sentence **(e)** that it is the first initiative of its kind. However, sentences **(f)** and **(g)** are both true.

> *Los representantes han confirmado que están seguros de que su programa <u>será exitoso</u> debido al éxito que ya han tenido iniciativas parecidas, por ejemplo <u>las reducciones en la cantidad de sal</u> y azúcar en ciertos alimentos <u>durante la última década</u>.*

Ya ha tenido mucho éxito ≠ será exitoso
Menos sal = reducciones en la cantidad de sal
Hace unos diez años = durante la última década

(h) *Los anuncios tienen una influencia dañina en la salud de los jóvenes.* – TRUE
(i) *El Gobierno es responsable de los anuncios.* – FALSE

We are told that adverts promote unhealthy food which contributes to child obesity (therefore sentence **(h)** is true) but it is not mentioned that the government is responsible, although it does want the food industry to reduce these adverts.

> *Otra <u>influencia negativa</u> en la obesidad entre <u>niños</u> es el montón de anuncios que promueven la comida poco saludable. El Gobierno quiere <u>que la industria alimentaria reduzca</u> estos anuncios.*

Influencia dañina = influencia negativa
Jóvenes = niños

(j) *Muchas compañías de comida rápida también proveen otras opciones que son mejores para la salud.* – TRUE
(k) *La ley requiere que todos productos alimenticios muestren la información nutricional.* – FALSE

Finally, we are told that many companies do now provide healthy options and nutritional information, although this is **not** yet required by law.

Muchas empresas ya ofrecen <u>opciones más saludables</u> y proveen información nutricional en los paquetes, pero hasta ahora <u>no hay legislación</u> para esto y queda mucho por recorrer.

Compañías = empresas
Opciones que son mejores para la salud = opciones más saludables
La ley requiere ≠ no hay legislación

Full transcript
F: *Como parte de una iniciativa para combatir la obesidad infantil, la cantidad de calorías en la comida basura se disminuirá dentro de un año. Estos cambios significarán que los supermercados y restaurantes de comida basura tendrán que reducir el tamaño de los productos o cambiar los ingredientes en la comida.*

Los representantes han confirmado que están seguros de que su programa será exitoso debido al éxito que ya han las tenido iniciativas parecidas, por ejemplo, las reducciones en la cantidad de sal y azúcar en ciertos alimentos durante la última década.

Otra influencia negativa en la obesidad entre niños es el montón de anuncios que promueven la comida poco saludable. El Gobierno quiere que la industria alimentaria reduzca estos anuncios. Muchas empresas ya ofrecen opciones más saludables y proveen información nutricional en los paquetes, pero hasta ahora no hay legislación para esto y queda mucho por recorrer.

Mark Scheme:

0-6	- Award one mark for each correct answer, up to six. - Deduct one mark for each incorrect answer, even if the correct answers are also crossed.

Entrevista con Ángela González

> **8 (a) Why are Ángela's achievements notable?**
>
> *Youngest player to be number one (in the youth rankings)*   [1]

Longer passages like this are designed to help the strongest candidates achieve top grades, and may contain unfamiliar words or terms. If you don't understand something that you hear, try and work it out from the context – see *TOP TIP: Write out words you don't know* in **Listening Paper 1**, **Question 7(b)(i)**.

Use the spaces to make other notes, but put your shorthand responses in the answer spaces to help you quickly remember the question, and also to prevent you from writing in the wrong section when you return to it. It would be near impossible to write everything down – see *TOP TIP: Make shorthand notes* in **Listening Paper 1**, **Question 7(a)**.

The relevant information comes right at the start of the piece:

> *Bueno, Ángela, felicidades. Eres **la tenista más joven en lograr la posición número uno** en el ranking juvenil nacional.*

Both parts of the answer are necessary for the full mark: her age is important, but you also need the fact that she is number one in the (youth) rankings.

Mark Scheme:

0/1	- Candidate has not identified the important information in the passage. - Candidate's translation is nonspecific, indicating guesswork.
1/1	- Candidate has identified and supplied the correct information: that she is the youngest player ever to achieve the number one ranking.

> **8 (b) What does she put her success down to? Give two ideas.**
>
> Any TWO of:
> *Her coach*   [1]
> *She has worked very hard*   [1]
> *She trains every day*   [1]
> *A bit of luck*   [1]

Ángela gives several reasons for her success, and you need to give two. She mentions her coach/trainer and that she has worked very hard, training every day. She also reveals that she thinks she had a bit of luck in the final. Any of those reasons would count towards a mark, although to be safe, it would be wise to separate training hard from training every day. In a different mark scheme, these may be judged to be too similar to each other to score a mark each. If you have more than two reasons, put them all to be sure of getting full marks, so long as it doesn't use up too much of your time.

> *Es fenomenal. Tengo un **entrenador** muy especial y **he trabajado muy duro** con él, **entrenando** todos los días. También tuve **un poco de suerte** en la final.*

Mark Scheme:

0/2	- Information is not supplied or not relevant.
1/2	- Candidate has identified and supplied one correct reason for her success.
2/2	- Candidate has identified and supplied two correct, separate reasons for her success.

> **8 (c) What are her immediate plans for the future?**
>
> *Rest/recharge her batteries*
> OR:
> *A holiday*   [1]

Ángela explicitly says that her main priority is to rest. She then expands that she is going to the United States with her family to recharge her batteries before the new season starts. This is all part of the same point, so any of this information would get the mark as long as it conveys the right message. A **wrong** interpretation would be that she is going to the United States for the start of the new season – this would be the opposite of a rest!

> *Bueno, primero de todo, necesito **descansar**. Voy a ir a los Estados Unidos con mi familia para <u>recargar las pilas</u> antes de que la nueva temporada empiece.*

Mark Scheme:

0/1	- Candidate has not identified the important information in the passage. - Candidate's translation is nonspecific, indicating guesswork.
1/1	- Candidate has identified and supplied the correct information: that she needs to rest.

---

8 (d) What does she feel is her greatest sporting moment?

Playing against Venus Williams/her idol [1]

In the build-up to answering this question, Ángela lists some of her other achievements, including winning regional tournaments (perfect tense) and representing her country next year (future tense). However, she then explicitly says that playing against Venus Williams was the moment she will always remember and was very special to her, even though she lost.

> *Sí, he ganado muchos torneos regionales y el año que viene estaré muy orgullosa de representar a mi país en un torneo internacional. Para mí, <u>el momento que siempre voy a conservar</u> es **cuando jugué contra Venus Williams**, que es mi ídolo. Perdí, claro, pero me resultó <u>muy especial</u>.*

Mark Scheme:

0/1	- Candidate has not identified the important information in the passage. - Candidate's translation is nonspecific, indicating guesswork.
1/1	- Candidate has identified and supplied the correct information: that her match against Venus Williams was her greatest sporting moment.

---

8 (e) What are her plans for life after tennis?

Coaching
OR:
Her own tennis academy [1]

Ángela's initial answer is that she is unsure, but she likes the idea of working with children. Given that she is a tennis player, being a coach or trainer would leap to mind as a possible future career. She then goes on to say that she thinks she would be a good coach and may open her own tennis academy. Either of these would suffice as an answer to gain the mark.

> *No sé exactamente pero, cuando me jubile, me apetece <u>trabajar con niños</u>. Creo que yo sería una buena **entrenadora** y posiblemente fundar **mi propia academia de tenis** para <u>niños que quieren mejorar</u>. Sin embargo, por ahora …*

Mark Scheme:

0/1	- Candidate has not identified the important information in the passage. - Candidate's translation is nonspecific, indicating guesswork.
1/1	- Candidate has identified and supplied the correct information about her plans for after tennis.

---

8 (f) What concerns her? Give two ideas.

Getting injured [1]
Not/never being able to have a normal life [1]

Ángela carries on from her previous point to her current concerns, introducing both things with two forms of *preocuparse*: firstly, *estoy preocupada por* and then *me preocupa*, which works like a *gustar*-type impersonal verb. The first thing she is worried about is getting injuries, and she then explains that she can't play well with an injury and needs to strengthen her body to avoid them. Even if you didn't know the words *herida* or *lesión*, this extra information may help you work them out from context. She also says she is worried she will never be able to lead a normal life, and that sometimes the only thing she wants to do is go to school and chat to her friends, but she can't as she has to train. Again, a succinct translation of this information would be enough to gain you the mark.

> *Sin embargo, por ahora quiero concentrarme en mantenerme en forma, porque **estoy muy preocupada por las heridas y lesiones**. <u>No podré jugar bien si tengo una lesión</u>, por eso necesito fortalecer mi cuerpo. También **me preocupa que nunca pueda tener una vida normal**. A veces, <u>lo único que quiero hacer es ir al insti y charlar con mis amigos</u>, pero no puedo, tengo que entrenar.*

Mark Scheme:

0/2	- Information is not supplied or not relevant.
1/2	- Candidate has identified and supplied one correct thing that concerns Ángela.
2/2	- Candidate has identified and supplied two correct, separate things that concern Ángela.

Full transcript

M: *Bueno, Ángela, felicidades. Eres la tenista más joven en lograr la posición número uno en el ranking juvenil nacional. ¿Cómo te sientes?*

F: *Es fenomenal. Tengo un entrenador muy especial y he trabajado muy duro con él, entrenando todos los días. También tuve un poco de suerte en la final.*

M: *No es verdad, jugaste muy bien. Y ahora, ¿qué?*

F: *Gracias. Bueno, primero de todo, necesito descansar. Voy a ir a los Estados Unidos con mi familia para recargar las pilas antes de que la nueva temporada empiece.*

M: *Ya has logrado tanto en tu vida… pero, ¿qué dirías que fue lo mejor?*

F: *Sí, he ganado muchos torneos regionales y el año que viene estaré muy orgullosa de representar a mi país en un torneo internacional. Para mí, el momento que siempre voy a conservar es cuando jugué contra Venus Williams, que es mi ídolo. Perdí, claro, pero me resultó muy especial.*

M: *¿Tienes planes para el futuro, aparte del tenis?*

F: *No sé exactamente, pero, cuando me jubile, me apetece trabajar con niños. Creo que yo sería una buena entrenadora y posiblemente fundar mi propia academia de tenis para niños que quieren mejorar. Sin embargo, por ahora quiero concentrarme en mantenerme en forma, porque estoy muy preocupada por las heridas y lesiones. No podré jugar bien si tengo una lesión, por eso necesito fortalecer mi cuerpo. También me preocupa que nunca pueda tener una vida normal. A veces, lo único que quiero hacer es ir al insti y charlar con mis amigos, pero no puedo, tengo que entrenar.*

La informática

> **9 (a) ¿Cuál es la estadística que preocupa a los expertos en informática?**
>
> *Las mujeres representan (menos del) 10% de estudiantes* [1]

The question asks you for a specific piece of information: a statistic. Listen out for a percentage, or a ratio, fraction or decimal. You are also told that the statistic is worrying, so the information you are looking for could have negative implications – in the recording, we are told that the statistic is worrying for the tech industry. The specific information is revealed in the opening sentence: that women make up less than ten percent of all IT/computing students.

> *Se ha revelado que, este año, **las mujeres representan menos del diez por ciento** de todos los estudiantes de informática - una estadística muy preocupante para la industria de tecnología.*

Mark Scheme:

0/1	- Candidate has not identified the important information in the passage. - Candidate has quoted indiscriminately from the recording, indicating guesswork.
1/1	- Candidate has identified and supplied the key statistic that less than 10% of IT students are female. - All answers in this section must be in Spanish.

> **9 (b) ¿Cómo es la situación en la industria en general?**
>
> *Menos mujeres/Falta de mujeres*
> OR:
> *Igual/parecida/semejante* [1]

Next, the speaker tells us that the figures from the last ten years show a lack of women in the tech industry in general. It is also possible to refer back to the answer in **9(a)** and say that the situation is similar or the same, although quoting the same statistic (less than 10%) would be incorrect, as this specifically referred to the study of IT students. You instead need to apply the information, to give a general overview of the situation in the industry.

> *Es más, las figuras de los últimos diez años muestran que **hay una falta de mujeres en la industria** tecnológica en general.*

Mark Scheme:

0/1	- Candidate has not identified the important information in the passage. - Candidate has quoted indiscriminately from the recording, indicating guesswork.
1/1	- Candidate has identified and supplied the correct information: that the situation within the industry is similar to the situation in question **(a)**.

> **9 (c) ¿Cuáles son las dos cosas que creen los expertos?**
>
> *Una falta de habilidades digitales* [1]
> *Una mezcla de mujeres y hombres es esencial* [1]

The recording explicitly introduces the correct information by stating that the experts agree on two things. You will need both parts of the answer to score full marks on this question: first, that there is a lack of digital skills and, secondly, that a mix of men and women is essential for advancements in the field. Paraphrasing in Spanish is fine as long as it conveys the same essential information e.g. *Debe haber un equilibrio entre los dos sexos*. Quoting directly and succinctly from the recording is also an acceptable method of conveying the correct answer, and may be a wiser strategy to make sure you are conveying the specific information. However, be sure not to quote too much from the text, as this may indicate you haven't understood the task.

> *Los expertos están de acuerdo sobre dos cosas: primero, **hay una falta de habilidades digitales** en el mundo; y segundo, **una mezcla de mujeres y hombres es esencial para avanzar**.*

Mark Scheme:

0/2	- Information is not supplied or not relevant.
1/2	- Candidate has identified and supplied one correct thing that the experts believe.
2/2	- Candidate has identified and supplied the two correct, separate things that the experts believe.

> **9 (d) ¿Por qué no hay sólo malas noticias?**
>
> *El número de chicas que estudian la informática ha aumentado*   [1]

Once again, you need to convey the key information: that the number of girls studying IT has increased. You can give the actual figure (30%), but it isn't strictly necessary if you have already identified the good news. The recording signals where the information will be with *sin embargo*, indicating a change in tone from the worrying and negative information given so far, and also explicitly calling it *la buena noticia*.

> *Sin embargo, la buena noticia es que **el número de chicas que estudian informática ha aumentado** en un 30% en el último año. Los jefes de las empresas digitales y tecnológicas esperan que este número siga aumentando …*

Mark Scheme:

0/1	- Candidate has not identified the important information in the passage. - Candidate has quoted indiscriminately from the recording, indicating guesswork.
1/1	- Candidate has identified and supplied the correct information: that the number of females studying IT/computing has increased.

> **9 (e) Da dos razones por las que las chicas no quieren estudiar la informática en el colegio.**
>
> Any TWO of:
> *Muchas (estudiantes) quieren ajustarse al estereotipo*   [1]
> *No quieren ser la única chica en su clase*   [1]
> *(Informática) es muy difícil*   [1]
> *Falta de confianza*   [1]

The key information for this section is given by the teacher, la señora López, although the male speaker paraphrases that many students try to conform to stereotypes, which would count as a reason. The teacher then gives more possible reasons, any of which would also score a mark: that girls don't want to be the only girl in their class; that there is a perception that the science subjects are very difficult and students who lack confidence won't choose them.

Again, you can give a third or fourth reason if you know them and want to be sure of getting full marks, but don't worry if not. Lead with the answers you are most confident with, as the examiner will read and reward these first, and may not even need to read the others if the first two reasons you give are correct.

> *Según la profesora de informática, sra. López, muchos estudiantes **quieren ajustarse al estereotipo**: "Muchas chicas no optan por esta asignatura porque **no quieren ser la única chica** en su clase. En los colegios de un único sexo, la participación de las chicas es mayor. **Hay una percepción de que las materias de ciencias son muy difíciles**, y los estudiantes a quienes **les falta confianza** no las elegirán. ..."*

Mark Scheme:

0/2	- Information is not supplied or not relevant.
1/2	- Candidate has identified and supplied one correct reason why girls might not choose to study IT.
2/2	- Candidate has identified and supplied the two correct, separate reasons why girls might not choose to study IT.

> **9 (f) Según la señora López, ¿qué necesita cambiar? Da una idea.**
>
> *La percepción de estas materias/asignaturas*
> OR:
> *Nuestros prejuicios (inconscientes)* [1]

La señora López concludes her short interview by saying that we need to change (*necesitamos cambiar* – the same wording as the question) the perception of these (science) subjects, as well as (using *además de* to link two similar ideas) our unconscious prejudices. You don't need both ideas to gain the mark; just one would do. You also don't need full sentences for any of the answers in this question, and again only one or two words here would suffice. Take notes throughout to help you.

> ... *"Por eso **necesitamos cambiar la percepción** de estas materias, además de **nuestros prejuicios inconscientes**."*

Mark Scheme:

0/1	- Candidate has not identified the important information in the passage. - Candidate has quoted indiscriminately from the recording, indicating guesswork.
1/1	- Candidate has identified and supplied one correct thing that la sra. López thinks needs to change.

Full transcript

M: *Se ha revelado que, este año, las mujeres representan menos del diez por ciento de todos los estudiantes de informática - una estadística muy preocupante para la industria de tecnología. Es más, las figuras de los últimos diez años muestran que hay una falta de mujeres en la industria tecnológica en general. Los expertos están de acuerdo sobre dos cosas: primero, hay una falta de habilidades digitales en el mundo, y segundo, una mezcla de mujeres y hombres es esencial para avanzar. Sin embargo, la buena noticia es que el número de chicas que estudian informática ha aumentado en un 30% en el último año. Los jefes de las empresas digitales y tecnológicas esperan que este número siga aumentando y que las chicas reconozcan que las ciencias de la computación son una buena opción para la Universidad y el mundo del trabajo, sin tener en cuenta si las han estudiado en el instituto. Según la profesora de informática, sra. López, muchos estudiantes quieren ajustarse al estereotipo:*

F: *"Muchas chicas no optan por esta asignatura porque no quieren ser la única chica en su clase. En los colegios de un único sexo, la participación de las chicas es mayor. Hay una percepción de que las asignaturas de ciencias son muy difíciles, y los estudiantes a quienes les falta confianza no las elegirán. Por eso necesitamos cambiar la percepción de estas materias, además de nuestros prejuicios inconscientes."*

END OF SOLUTIONS FOR PAPER 3

Listening Paper 4

> *Visit **www.rsleducational.co.uk/spanishaudio** to download the audio file for this paper.*

If you wish to complete this paper in timed conditions, allow 45 minutes plus 5 minutes' reading time.

Instructions

- Use **black** ink or ballpoint pen.
- Answer **all** questions.
- Answer the questions in the spaces provided.
    - *There may be more space than you require.*
- Dictionaries are **not** allowed.

Advice

- You have 5 minutes to read through the paper before the recording starts.
- You will hear each extract twice. You may write at any time during the examination. There will be a pause between each question.
- Read each question **carefully** before attempting it.
- The marks available for each question are given in [square brackets]. These give you an indication of how long to spend on each question.
- There is a total of **50 marks** available for this paper.
- Leave time to check your answers at the end, if possible.

Answer ALL questions.

Mi vida

1   Agustín habla sobre su vida. ¿Qué cuatro cosas menciona? Pon una equis [X] en cada casilla correcta.

Agustín is talking about his life. Which **four** things does he mention? Put a cross **[X]** in each correct box.

(Total for Question 1 = 4 marks)

Mi pueblo

2   Estos amigos hablan sobre su pueblo. ¿De qué lugares hablan? Pon una equis
     [X] en cada casilla correcta.

     These friends are talking about their town. Which places are they talking
     about? Put a cross [X] in each correct box.

-   Gimnasio -   Colegio -   ~~Museo~~ -   Biblioteca -   Cine -   Parque -   Teatro -   Discoteca -   Bar

Ejemplo: Matías	Museo
(a) Paula	
(b) Javier	
(c) Ana	
(d) Santi	
(e) Jorge	

(Total for Question 2 = 5 marks)

En el hotel

3   Vas a la recepción de tu hotel. ¿Qué te dicen? Pon una equis **[X]** en cada casilla correcta.

You go to the reception in your hotel. What do they tell you? Put a cross **[X]** in each correct box.

(a) ¿Qué número es tu habitación?

(i)	(ii)	(iii)
3	23	20

(b) ¿En qué planta está tu habitación?

(i)	(ii)	(iii)
2	3	4

(c) ¿A qué hora es el desayuno?

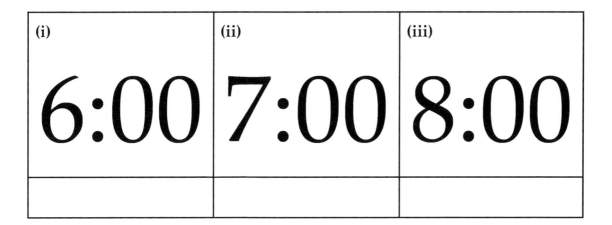

(i)	(ii)	(iii)
6:00	7:00	8:00

(d) ¿Cómo puedes ir a la playa?

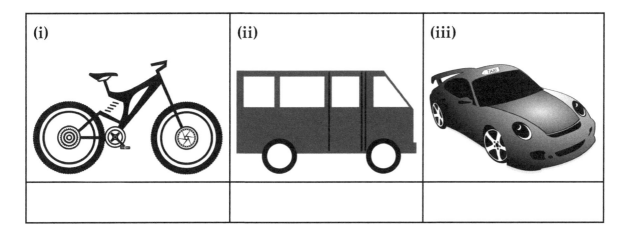

(i)	(ii)	(iii)

(e) ¿Dónde está la piscina?

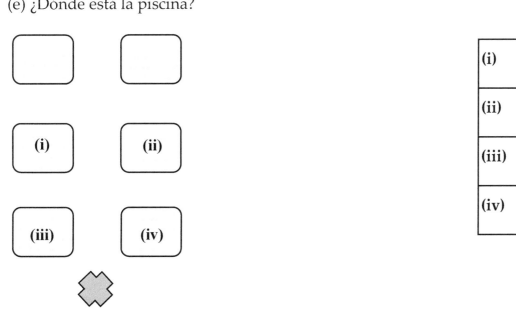

(i)	
(ii)	
(iii)	
(iv)	

(i)	(ii)
(iii)	(iv)

Estás aquí

(Total for Question 3 = 5 marks)

Fiesta de cumpleaños

4   Escucha esta conversación entre dos amigos. Luego, pon la(s) letra(s) correcta(s) en cada casilla para indicar si las afirmaciones son verdaderas o falsas o si no se menciona.

Listen to this conversation between two friends. Then put the appropriate letter(s) in each box to indicate whether the information is true, false, or not mentioned.

Verdadero = V
Falso = F
No se menciona = NM

Ejemplo: El lunes es el cumpleaños de Marta.	F
(a) Habrá una fiesta en casa de Marta.	
(b) La fiesta empieza a las nueve.	
(c) Juan tiene que limpiar el cuarto de baño.	
(d) La hermana de Juan es mayor que él.	
(e) Habrá alcohol disponible en la fiesta.	
(f) El padre de Juan es abogado.	

(Total for Question 4 = 6 marks)

Trabajos

5   Estas personas están hablando sobre trabajos. ¿Cuáles son sus trabajos ideales y cuáles trabajos tienen actualmente?

These people are talking about jobs. What are their ideal jobs, and what jobs do they currently have?

(a)

Ideal job	Current Job
	Ejemplo: Engineer

(b)

Ideal job	Current Job

(c)

Ideal job	Current Job

(d)

Ideal job	Current Job

(Total for Question 5 = 7 marks)

Mi familia

6   ¿Qué piensan estas personas de sus familias? Escribe la(s) letra(s) correcta(s) en cada casilla para indicar si sus opiniones son **positivas**, **negativas**, o **las dos.**

What do these people think of their families? Write the appropriate letter(s) in each box to indicate whether their opinions are **positive**, **negative**, or **both**.

P (Positive)
N (Negative)
P+N (Positive + Negative)

(a) Gloria	
(b) Joaquín	
(c) Carla	

(Total for Question 6 = 3 marks)

¿Estudiar en el extranjero?

7   Estas personas están discutiendo la importancia de estudiar en el extranjero. Escribe **en español** en la tabla las razones por las que se debe ir a la universidad en el extranjero, y aquellas por las que no. No tienes que escribir frases completas, pero debes usar cada casilla disponible.

These people are discussing the importance of studying abroad. Write **in Spanish** in the grid below the reasons why one should go to university abroad and the reasons one shouldn't. You don't have to write in full sentences but you should use every available box.

Razones para estudiar en el extranjero
Ejemplo: Nuevas perspectivas del mundo

Razones para no estudiar en el extranjero

(Total for Question 7 = 4 marks)

Entrevista a un periodista

8   Escucha esta entrevista a un periodista y luego contesta las preguntas que están debajo **en inglés**. No tienes que escribir frases completas.

Listen to this interview with a journalist, and then answer the questions below **in English**. You don't have to write full sentences.

(a) Why is this an interesting time to be a journalist? [1]

....

(b) Why do people become journalists? Give **two** reasons. [2]

....

....

(c) According to el señor Montero, what is the duty of a journalist? [1]

....

(d) What has been the best moment of his career? [1]

....

(e) What do journalists nowadays need for their careers? Give **two** ideas. [2]

....

....

(f) What are his plans for after retirement? Give **one** idea. [1]

....

(Total for Question 8 = 8 marks)

Trenes chinos

9   Escucha esta grabación sobre los trenes de alta velocidad. Luego, contesta las preguntas que están debajo **en español**. No tienes que escribir frases completas.

Listen to this recording about high-speed trains. Then answer the questions below **in Spanish**. You don't have to write full sentences.

(a) ¿Cuánto tiempo toma **actualmente** ir desde Shanghaí hasta Beijing?   [1]

....

(b) ¿Por qué pusieron un límite de velocidad en los trenes?   [1]

....

(c) ¿Cuál es la velocidad media de los nuevos trenes?   [1]

....

(d) ¿Cuál es la función del nuevo sistema de control?   [1]

....

(e) Aparte del sistema de emergencia, ¿qué otros cambios hay para mejorar la experiencia de los pasajeros? Da **dos** ideas.   [2]

....

....

(f) ¿Cuáles fueron los resultados de los choques de 2011? Da **dos** ideas. [2]

. . . .

(Total for Question 9 = 8 marks)

TOTAL FOR PAPER = 50 MARKS

_____

Blank Page

Listening Paper 4 – SOLUTIONS

Mi vida

---

1 Agustín habla sobre su vida. ¿Qué cuatro cosas menciona?

(b) (c) (f) (h) [4]

In this simple "warm-up" question, you are required to put a cross underneath the pictures once you hear the Spanish word(s) in the dialogue. The GCSE vocabulary being tested here is lifestyle (*mi vida*).

You need to cross **exactly** four boxes! Remember to make notes in pencil to begin with and neatly cross out each picture once you have used it, so you know not to use it again. Listen out for the four things about his life that Agustín mentions. The answers will not necessarily occur in the recording in the same order as the pictures and not everything he says will have a corresponding picture.

For example, as well as his house, he mentions his parents (who are both teachers). There isn't a matching picture for this information but there is a picture of a doctor, which he says is what he wants to be. Although he is generally unhealthy, he does get some exercise when he walks the dog. There is also an image of music, but that isn't what he uses the radio for.

Full transcript – the answers are given in **bold**.

M: *Hola, me llamo Agustín. Vivo en una **casa** grande en las afueras de Sevilla con mis padres. Son profesores, pero yo quiero ser **médico**. No soy muy sano. La única forma de ejercicio que hago es cuando tengo que **pasear al perro**. Sin embargo, me gusta ver el fútbol en la **tele** o escucharlo en la radio.*

Mark Scheme:

0-4	- Award one mark for each correct answer, up to four. - Deduct one mark for each incorrect answer, even if the correct answers are also crossed. *- Therefore, crossing eight boxes would mean four wrong answers and score 0 marks.*

Mi pueblo

---

2 ¿De qué lugares hablan?

    (a) *Paula – Colegio*   [1]
    (b) *Javier – Bar*   [1]
    (c) *Ana – Biblioteca*   [1]
    (d) *Santi – Teatro*   [1]
    (e) *Jorge – Parque*   [1]

In this exercise, you are expected to listen and work out from context each of the places that are mentioned. Again, make notes in pencil if necessary, and put a neat line through the words that have already been used, like *museo* in the example.

Listen out for clues and vocabulary, and don't stop listening once you think you have heard the right word – there may be traps! See *TOP TIP: Pay attention to the whole sentence* in **Listening Paper 1, Question 2**.

After Matías in the example has talked about his fascination with history musems, Paula **(a)** says this is boring and compares it to history class because she can't stand her school. Even if you didn't know that *insti* is short for *instituto*, which is a synonym of *colegio*, the mention of history class would be enough of a clue to give you the answer.

Javier **(b)** agrees and says that he likes going for beers with friends and relaxing – so a *bar*. Ana **(c)** says that going out every night is too expensive and she prefers to rent a film (*alquilar* is both to rent/borrow and – the opposite – to lend). So, despite her mention of films, she is in fact talking about the *biblioteca*, not the *cine* – because it is cheaper than going out! Santi **(d)** then disagrees with this because he prefers the <u>live</u> experience, and so likes to go to see theatre shows. Finally, Jorge **(e)** disagrees with them all. He likes doing exercise, but rather than going to the *gimnasio*, he goes running in the fresh air near his house – so to the *parque*.

Full transcript

Ejemplo: M: *En mi tiempo libre me encanta nada más que ir al* **museo** *de historia. Lo encuentro fascinante, y puedo aprender un montón.*

(a) F: *Pero, Matías, ¡qué aburrido! Será como una clase de historia, y yo no puedo aguantar mi* **insti**.

(b) M: *Yo estoy de acuerdo con Paula. En mi tiempo libre me gusta ir a* **tomar unas cervezas** *con mis amigos y estar tranquilo. ¿Qué crees tú, Ana?*

(c) F: *Para mí, es demasiado caro salir cada noche. Yo* **prefiero alquilar una película**, *es mucho más barato.*

(d) M: *Pero eso no es tan emocionante como experimentar el ambiente en vivo. Por eso, yo prefiero ir a **obras de teatro**. ¿Y tú, Jorge?*

(e) M: *Todas esas opciones suenan muy raras. A mí me gusta hacer ejercicio y, por lo tanto, voy a **correr al aire libre** cerca de mi casa.*

Mark Scheme:

0-5	- Award one mark for each correct answer. - Incorrect or multiple answers do not score.

En el hotel

3 Vas a la recepción en tu hotel. ¿Qué te dicen?	
(a) *(iii)*	[1]
(b) *(ii)*	[1]
(c) *(ii)*	[1]
(d) *(i)*	[1]
(e) *(iv)*	[1]

This question tests your ability to cope with a large amount of information at once and pinpoint the important parts. Therefore, it may be necessary to make notes in pencil throughout the recording, and then erase or edit if you change your mind – see *TOP TIP: Make shorthand notes* in **Listening Paper 1, Question 7(a)**.

Make sure you have read the questions before the recording starts, so you know the information you are listening for and are able to identify it when you hear it. The receptionist tells you that your key is for room 20 on the third floor, which is the answer to the questions **(a)** and **(b)**. Then she says the kitchen is open for breakfast from 7am. 8am is also mentioned but that is the time from which coaches to the beach start (*autocar* is commonly mistaken for car, when it means coach). Finally, there is a simple direction to the pool: the first door on the right.

Full transcript

F: *Bienvenido, señor González. Aquí tiene su llave para la habitación número **veinte** en el **tercer** piso. Si quiere desayunar, la cocina está abierta desde las **siete**. Y desde las ocho en punto habrá un **autocar** para la playa cada hora. De momento, se puede relajar en la piscina que está allí, por **la primera puerta a la derecha**.*

Mark Scheme:

0-5	- Award one mark for each correct answer, up to five. - Incorrect or multiple answers do not score.

Fiesta de cumpleaños

> **4 (a) Habrá una fiesta en casa de Marta.**
> *V*   [1]
>
> **(b) La fiesta empieza a las nueve.**
> *NM*   [1]
>
> **(c) Juan tiene que limpiar el cuarto de baño.**
> *F*   [1]
>
> **(d) La hermana de Juan es mayor que él.**
> *F*   [1]
>
> **(e) Habrá alcohol disponible en la fiesta.**
> *V*   [1]
>
> **(f) El padre de Juan es abogado.**
> *NM*   [1]

In this exercise, you have to listen to the recording to determine whether the corresponding sentences are true or false – or the information in the sentence may not be mentioned at all! Again, make notes in pencil so you can change your answers if you have to. Most importantly, **read the sentences** before the recording starts so you know what to listen out for. You may not understand everything, but your notes should still help you to work out the answer.

The example sentence is that Marta's birthday on Monday, but the recording says it is on Friday (*viernes*). Marta does say that she is having a party at her house **(a)**, but does not mention the start time **(b)**. Juan then says he will arrive late because he is cleaning his own room, not the bathroom (*cuarto de baño*) so **(c)** is false. His sister is younger not older **(d)**, so can't come because there will be *cerveza y vino* (= alcohol) **(e)**. Juan therefore says he will ask his father to look after her, if he's not working, but he doesn't mention what his job is – so **(f)** is *NM*.

Full transcript

M: *Oye, Marta. Es tu cumpleaños este viernes, ¿verdad?*

F: *Hola Juan. Sí, haré una fiesta en mi casa. ¿Vendrás?*

M: *Claro, pero voy a llegar tarde. Mis padres dicen que tengo que limpiar mi cuarto. ¿Puedo traer a mi hermana pequeña? Tiene quince años.*

F: *Creo que no. No será apropiada para ella. Tomaremos mucha cerveza y vino.*

M: *Bueno, no importa. Preguntaré a mi padre para que la cuide, si no está trabajando.*

Mark Scheme:

0-6	- Award one mark for each correct answer, up to six. - Incorrect, or multiple answers do not score.

Trabajos	
5 (a) Ideal Job – *Pilot*	[1]
(b) Ideal Job – *(Children's) author/writer*	[1]
Current job – *Hairdresser*	[1]
(c) Ideal Job – *Lawyer*	[1]
Current job – *Unemployed/No job*	[1]
(d) Ideal Job – *Actor/actress*	[1]
Current job – *Nurse*	[1]

As the title of this question suggests, you are being tested on your knowledge of jobs and the world of work. Use your knowledge of this vocabulary and any notes you have taken to work out which jobs each person is talking about. You also have to work out which job they currently do, and which would be their ideal job. Therefore, just like the questions in which you have to identify positive or negative opinions, listen out for adjectives and adverbs which convey these – see *TOP TIP: Find positive/negative opinions* in **Listening Paper 3**, **Question 6**.

In addition, descriptions of people's current jobs are most likely to be in the present or present continuous (*estar* + present participle) tense or use a temporal phrase such as *en este momento, hoy en día* or *actualmente*. By contrast, **ideal** jobs are likely to be in the conditional or future tenses.

As you can tell from the example, one- or two-word answers **in English** are expected, so don't write too much (in other words, be specific). Paco works as an engineer for a company that manufactures aeroplanes, but says it is boring (*aburrido*). He contrasts this with being a pilot: *sería mucho más interesante* – using the conditional tense, with a positive adjective (*interesante*) and qualifying adverbs (*mucho más*). The second voice **(b)** follows a similar structure: she currently works for her mum as a hairdresser, but it **isn't** her ideal job – don't be fooled! She switches from the present to the conditional tense to talk about her ideal job: she would prefer to be creative and write books for children. The part about being creative isn't necessary and it also wouldn't suffice on its own (being creative isn't a job, unfortunately!), so this would be an example of writing too much. "Write (children's) books", or simply "(children's) author" would be fine as answers.

The next voice **(c)** says he studied law at university and now can't understand why he can't get a good job as a lawyer. This information, as well as the positive description of law as *un buen trabajo*, tells us that this is his ideal job, rather than being unemployed – *estar en paro* is a synonym of *desempleado*, meaning unemployed. Finally, **(d)** begins by telling us that her ideal job is being a star and acting in films, but realises this isn't very realistic. Therefore, she will keep working in the hospital as a nurse: *seguir* + present participle means to continue doing something.

Full transcript
(a) *Hola, soy Paco. Trabajo como **ingeniero** para una compañia que fabrica aviones, pero el trabajo es muy aburrido. Sería mucho más interesante ser el **piloto**.*
(b) *En este momento, trabajo para mi madre como **peluquera**, pero no es mi trabajo ideal. Preferiría ser creativa y **escribir libros** para niños.*
(c) *Yo estudié Derecho en la Universidad, así que no puedo entender por qué no puedo conseguir un buen trabajo como **abogado** en vez de estar **en paro**.*
(d) *¿Mi trabajo ideal? Bueno, me gustaría ser una **estrella** y **actuar** en las películas, pero sé que mi sueño no es muy realista. Por eso, sigo trabajando en el hospital como **enfermera**.*

Mark Scheme:

0-7	- Award one mark for each correct answer, up to seven.
	- Incorrect or multiple answers do not score.
	- One or two word answers are expected.

Mi familia

6 (a) *P* [1]
(b) *P+N* [1]
(c) *P* [1]

Similarly to **Question 5** in this paper, here you need to identify positive or negative opinions. Listen out for positive/negative descriptions as well as absolutes (*nunca*/*siempre*/*todo* etc.). There is some useful vocabulary in this exercise to express whether you do or don't get along with someone.

For example, the first speaker **(a)** says that they never (*nunca*) argue in her family; they get on very well and always (*siempre*) support each other. *Llevarse bien/mal* means to get on well/badly with, as does *caerse bien/mal*. Therefore, her opinion of her family is undoubtedly *positiva*.

The voice in **(b)** says that all familes have problems and his don't often (*a menudo*) agree (*estar de acuerdo*) but that they always make up afterwards. This would suggest a positive and negative (balanced) opinion.

Finally, the speaker in **(c)** reveals that she doesn't understand familes that fight all the time, and that in her family there is nothing but love and understanding. You might hear the phrase *pelearse todo el tiempo* or *nada* (*más que amor*) and think she is giving a negative or mixed opinion, but in fact it is positive.

Full transcript
F: *Nunca discutimos en nuestra familia. Nos llevamos muy bien y siempre nos apoyamos los unos a los otros.*
M: *Todas las familias tienen problemas. Nosotros no estamos de acuerdo a menudo, pero siempre hacemos las paces después.*
F: *No entiendo a las familias que se pelean todo el tiempo. En mi familia no hay nada más que amor y comprensión.*

Estudiar en el extranjero

---

7 Razones para estudiar en el extranjero

Any TWO, in any order:
Hacer amigos de diferentes partes del mundo/para toda la vida
OR:
Conocer a gente nueva de diferentes partes del mundo [1]

Aprender/Mejorar un nuevo idioma [1]

Razones para no ir estudiar en el extranjero

Any TWO, in any order:
Estar muy lejos de tus amigos
OR:
Echar de menos a tus amigos [1]

Muy caro/Cuesta demasiado/Los costes se acumulan [1]

[Maximum 4]

This is another long passage of dialogue, in which you have to pick out and write down both positive and negative reasons for studying abroad (two of each). The best approach is to make shorthand notes throughout and then fill in the gaps in your notes during the pauses – see *TOP TIP: Make shorthand notes* in **Listening Paper 1**, **Question 7(a)**. You have to write **in Spanish**, but remember, you don't have to write in full sentences.

Look out for words that introduce **opinions**, such as *en mi opinión, según yo, a mi parecer, pienso/creo/opino que*, or a **counter-argument**, such as *pero, sin embargo, no obstante, (no) estoy de acuerdo, (no) es verdad* – compare this to *TOP TIP: Look for opinions* in **Listening Paper 1**, **Question 8** as well as *TOP TIP: Find positive/negative opinions* in **Listening Paper 3**, **Question 6**.

Make sure that what you write are actually **reasons** – simply saying *es fantástico* or *te asusta* are **unjustified** opinions. The reasons in the recording don't necessarily occur in an ABAB order – there might be two negatives in the same sentence! Ensure that the reasons you give are different: for example, *conocer a gente nueva* and *hacer nuevos amigos* are essentially the same point and would only score one mark between them. Likewise, the female speaker's point that she would be so far away from her friends, and that she would miss them, would only count towards one mark. Regard these as clues towards the same point, rather than as separate reasons. For example, the fact that the male speaker says his English has improved since being in the United States is evidence that it is easier to learn a new language by studying abroad. The idea that costs accumulate is another way of saying that it is very expensive, rather than a separate point.

Full transcript

F: *¡Ramón! Hace dos años que no te veo, ¿cómo estás?*

M: *Muy bien, gracias Liliana. Estoy estudiando en los Estados Unidos. Es fantástico porque **te da nuevas perspectivas** del mundo.*

F: *¡Qué bueno! Pero, ¿no te asusta? A mí no me gustaría **estar tan lejos de mis amigas. Las echaría mucho de menos.***

M: *Al principio sí. Pero **se puede conocer a gente nueva** que está en la misma situación y **hacer amigos** de diferentes partes del mundo y para toda la vida.*

F: *Supongo que tienes razón. Sin embargo, puede resultar **muy caro**, ¿verdad? Los costes se acumulan muy rápidamente.*

M: *Sí, pero es así dondequiera que estudies, en mi opinión. La gran ventaja es que mi nivel de inglés ha aumentado como tú no creerías. Es mucho **más fácil aprender un nuevo idioma** así que en un aula.*

Mark Scheme:

0-4	- Award one mark for each correct reason given, up to four. - Each answer must contain clearly separate information, not repeat the same point using different words. - Incorrect or repeated answers do not score.

Entrevista a un periodista

8 (a) Why is this an interesting time to be a journalist? *More newspapers and news programmes* OR: *24-hour news channels* [1]

You may find it useful to take shorthand notes (don't try and write everything down!) during longer passages such as this one. There may be words and terms you are unfamiliar with, but it will often be possible to work out their meanings from the context. Any notes you make can be used to help you quickly remember the question, and also to prevent you from writing in the wrong section when you return to it. Remember to answer in English and to make sure that your answers are precise and accurately reflect the recording – see *TOP TIP: Be specific* in **Listening Paper 1**, **Question 9(a)**.

The language used to introduce the relevant information echoes the wording of the question:

> *Es* <u>*un tiempo interesante*</u>*. Hay* **cada vez más periódicos y programas de noticias**, *además de* **varios canales de noticias que transmiten 24 horas al día**. *Siempre hay algo nuevo que informar.*

There is one mark available for this question, so you only need to give one legitimate reason for the assertion: *es un tiempo interesante*. El señor Montero claims that it is an interesting time to be a journalist because of the increased demand for news content. Specifically, he says that there are an increasing number of newspaper and news programmes, as well as news channels that broadcast 24-hours a day. Either of these reasons would be enough to gain you the mark.

Mark Scheme:

0/1	- Candidate has not identified the important information in the passage. - Candidate's translation is nonspecific, indicating guesswork.
1/1	- Candidate has identified and supplied the correct information, conveying that there is more demand for news because of 24-hour broadcasting OR because of more newspapers and news programmes.

8 (b) Why do people become journalists? Give two reasons.	
For the love of writing	[1]
To mix with/report on celebrities	[1]

The necessary information in the recording occurs sequentially, and the information for question **(b)** immediately follows the information for **(a)**. The speaker says that are two reasons for becoming a journalist: for the love of writing, or because you want to mix with celebrities and write about their activities. Use your notes to help you understand the context, as he gives both reasons within a short space of time. He also says he belongs to the first group – but the second option is also important. You need both parts of the answer to gain full marks: the question asks for **two** reasons.

> *Hay <u>dos razones</u> por las que uno quisiera hacerse periodista: por **el amor a escribir** o porque **quieren mezclarse con celebridades** y escribir sobre sus actividades. A mí me encanta escribir, pero la segunda opción también es importante.*

Mark Scheme:

0/2	- Information is not supplied or not relevant.
1/2	- Candidate has identified and supplied one correct reason why people would want to become journalists.
2/2	- Candidate has identified and supplied the two correct reasons why people would want to become journalists.

8 (c) According to el señor Montero, what is the duty of a journalist?

To inform the public of the activities/opinions of politicians/corporations/sportspeople/ celebrities (only one needed)　　　　　　　　　　　　　　　　　　　[1]

El señor Montero follows up his position in question **(b)** with this opinion:

> *Yo opino que los periodistas tienen la responsabilidad **de informar al público sobre las opiniones y actividades de los políticos, las corporaciones, sus deportistas favoritos, etc.***

There simply isn't time to write all of this down, so make notes and then paraphrase your answer quickly. You only have to name one of the groups of people that Montero mentions (e.g. politicians) in order to gain the mark, so don't waste time writing them all down – pick the one you judge to be most important.

Mark Scheme:

0/1	- Candidate has not identified the important information in the passage. - Candidate's translation is nonspecific, indicating guesswork.
1/1	- Candidate has identified and supplied the correct information to convey Montero's opinion of a journalist's duty.

8 (d) What has been the best moment of his career?

Meeting the US President [1]

The interviewer then asks the question:

¿Le importan mucho los premios?

… to which Montero replies that he has won prizes in his life, but (unlike some other journalists) he doesn't care about them – he doesn't even know where they are now! He says that memories are more important to him, and the nicest memory of his career was when he met the President of the USA. Remember that Spanish speakers will often say *los Estados Unidos* (or *EE.UU*), rather than *América*, to refer to the USA, because *América* could also refer to Latin America. There is a long build-up before the answer to question **(d)** is revealed, so don't get distracted by talk of prizes or memories – the question asks for a specific moment.

No mucho. He ganado varios premios en mi vida, pero no sé donde están ahora. Los recuerdos son <u>más importantes</u> para mí. <u>El momento más especial</u> de mi carrera fue **cuando conocí al presidente de los Estados Unidos**. *Los periodistas de hoy se preocupan demasiado por los premios …*

Mark Scheme:

0/1	- Candidate has not identified the important information in the passage. - Candidate's translation is nonspecific, indicating guesswork.
1/1	- Candidate has identified and supplied the correct information: that the best moment of his career was meeting the President of the USA.

8 (e) What do journalists nowadays need for their career? Give two ideas.

Any TWO of:
An open mind
Patience
An aptitude/tendency for telling the truth
A (good) computer
A notebook [2]

Montero then immediately goes on to list the things which it is more important for journalists to have than awards. This list ranges from attributes to actual possessions, and you need to write down two clearly different things to get both marks for this question. As ever, if you do have a third correct option, write it down for safety, as long as doesn't take up too much time (restrict your answers to two or three words). Remember the *TOP TIP: Keep your points distinct*, from **Listening Paper 2, Question 8(b)**.

> *Los periodistas de hoy se preocupan demasiado por los premios, pero es mucho más importante tener* **una mente abierta***, mucha* **paciencia** *y* **una aptitud para decir la verdad***. Además de* **un buen ordenador** *y* **una libreta para notas***, por supuesto.*

Mark Scheme:

0/2	- Information is not supplied or not relevant.
1/2	- Candidate has identified and supplied one correct thing that a good journalist needs.
2/2	- Candidate has identified and supplied two correct things that a good journalist needs.

---

8 (f) What are his plans for after retirement? Give one idea.

Spend more time with grandchildren
OR:
Work/volunteer in a bookshop [1]

The information for this final question **(f)** is introduced specifically by the interviewer. Montero then responds that his plan for after he retires in two months is to spend more time with his grandchildren. *Nietos* is commonly mistranslated by English speakers as 'nieces and nephews', possibly because of the similarities in spelling, but it actually means 'grandchildren'. He also says that he wants to volunteer in a bookshop because he still loves the written word. Another common source of confusion is that *librería* means bookshop – a place that sells *libros* – and **not** library, which would be *biblioteca*. A correct translation of either of Montero's plans would gain the mark. Simply saying that he plans to retire would not – that information is already provided in the question!

F: *Y finalmente, ¿cuáles son sus planes para el futuro?*

M: *Dado que me jubilo dentro de dos meses, quiero pasar más tiempo con mis nietos. También voy a trabajar como voluntario en una librería, porque todavía me encanta la palabra escrita.*

Mark Scheme:

0/1	- Candidate has not identified the important information in the passage. - Candidate's translation is nonspecific, indicating guesswork.
1/1	- Candidate has identified and supplied the correct information about Montero's plans for the future.

Full transcript

F: *Buenos días, señor Montero. ¿Cómo es ser un periodista en estos momentos?*

M: *Es un tiempo interesante. Hay cada vez más periódicos y programas de noticias, además de varios canales de noticias que transmiten 24 horas al día. Siempre hay algo nuevo que informar. Hay dos razones por las que uno quisiera hacerse periodista: por el amor a escribir, o porque quieren mezclarse con celebridades y escribir sobre sus actividades. A mí me encanta escribir, pero la segunda opción también es importante. Yo opino que los periodistas tienen la responsabilidad de informar al público sobre las opiniones y actividades de los políticos, las corporaciones, sus deportistas favoritos, etc.*

F: *¿Le importan mucho los premios?*

M: *No mucho. He ganado varios premios en mi vida, pero no sé donde están ahora. Los recuerdos son más importantes para mí. El momento más lindo de mi carrera fue cuando conocí al presidente de los Estados Unidos. Los periodistas de hoy se preocupan demasiado por los premios, pero es mucho más importante tener una mente abierta, mucha paciencia, y una aptitud para decir la verdad. Además de un buen ordenador y una libreta para notas, por supuesto.*

F: *Y finalmente, ¿cuáles son sus planes para el futuro?*

M: *Dado que me jubilo dentro de dos meses, quiero pasar más tiempo con mis nietos. También voy a trabajar como voluntario en una librería, porque todavía me encanta la palabra escrita.*

Trenes chinos

9 (a) ¿Cuánto tiempo toma actualmente ir desde Shanghái hasta Beijing?	
Cinco horas	[1]

The final questions are designed to test the strongest GCSE candidates and are deliberately supposed to be tricky. In this question, you are asked to listen and respond **in Spanish**. You don't have to write in full sentences, so take notes where useful, and then write your answers during a pause in the recording, based on your notes and logic.

The recording takes the form of a news bulletin, and introduces the topic in the first sentence (as well as in the title of the section): a new high-speed rail network in China. The vital information for **(a)** occurs in the second sentence: you are told that the new trains will travel from Shanghai to Beijing in three and a half hours, which is an hour and a half **less** than they currently take. The key word here is *actualmente* (currently), rather than the new journey time, which is given in the future tense. Therefore, the answer is five hours.

> *Una mayor velocidad significará que el viaje desde Shanghái a Beijing* <u>durará</u> **tres horas y media, una hora y media** <u>*menos que actualmente*</u>.

Mark Scheme:

0/1	- Candidate has not identified the important information in the passage. - Candidate's translation is nonspecific or guesswork.
1/1	- Candidate has identified and supplied the correct information: that the current journey time is **five** hours.

9 (b) ¿Por qué pusieron un límite a de la velocidad de los trenes?	
Dos choques fatales/Cuarenta personas murieron	[1]

The speaker then mentions that the government limited the speed of these trains in 2011 following two crashes in which 40 people died. There is a little room for personal interpretation in your answer, but the key information is that these accidents and deaths were the trigger for new laws.

> *En 2011, <u>la velocidad</u> de estos trenes <u>fue limitada</u> por el Gobierno, después de **dos choques que mataron a cuarenta personas**.*

Mark Scheme:

0/1	- Candidate has not identified the important information in the passage. - Candidate's translation is nonspecific or guesswork.
1/1	- Candidate has identified and supplied the correct information: that the fatal crashes led to the government imposing a speed limit on the trains.

> **9 (c) ¿Cuál es la velocidad media de los nuevos trenes?**
>
> *350 kmh*   [1]

Question **(c)** requires a specific answer, so you must give a speed. The recording says that the new trains will have an average speed of 350 km/h, and engineers believe they could travel as fast as 400 km/h with improvements to the tracks. However, this second part is extraneous information – the **average speed** (repeated in the question) is *350 kilómetros por hora* (remember to give the units!).

> *Los nuevos trenes <u>viajarán</u> <u>a una velocidad media</u> de **350 kilómetros por hora** y los ingenieros creen que podrían ser aun más rápidos con mejoras en las vías, hasta 400 km/h.*

Mark Scheme:

0/1	- Candidate has not identified the important information in the passage. - Candidate's translation is nonspecific or guesswork.
1/1	- Candidate has identified and supplied the correct average speed of the trains.

> **9 (d) ¿Cuál es la función del nuevo sistema de control?**
>
> *Reducir la velocidad (automáticamente) (en caso de emergencia)*   [1]

The information you are required to find in this question is the specific function of the new control system, which is to reduce the speed of the trains automatically in case of emergency. You would get the mark if you simply wrote *reducir la velocidad*, as this does answer the question. However, you have to convey that the new system **reduces** the speed of the trains; "controlling" the speed isn't quite accurate enough, and could have been inferred from the question before you had even heard the recording.

---

*Tendrán <u>un sistema de control</u> que **reducirá la velocidad** automáticamente en caso de emergencia.*

Mark Scheme:

0/1	- Candidate has not identified the important information in the passage. - Candidate's translation is nonspecific or guesswork.
1/1	- Candidate has identified and supplied the correct function of the new control system.

---

9 (e) Aparte del sistema de emergencia, ¿qué otros cambios hay para mejorar la experiencia de los pasajeros? Da dos ideas.

Any TWO of:
Más confort/cómodo/comodidad
Más espacio (para las piernas)
Comida caliente
Internet (gratis)   [2]

Question **(e)** then asks you for two further improvements **apart from** the new emergency control system mentioned in question **(d)**. The recording gives a list of changes in addition to (*además de*) this system. Make sure that these changes are indeed improvements for the passengers, rather than being unnecessary, or changes for the worse. You could choose any TWO from: increased comfort, more (leg) room, hot food, and free internet access.

---

*Además de esto, habrá un **aumento de confort** para los pasajeros, con **más espacio para las piernas, comida caliente** y **acceso gratis a Internet**.*

Mark Scheme:

0/2	- Information is not supplied or not relevant.
1/2	- Candidate has identified and supplied one further correct improvement to the trains **apart from** the new emergency control system.
2/2	- Candidate has identified and supplied the two separate correct improvements to the trains apart from the new emergency control system.

---

9 (f) ¿Qué fueron los resultados de los choques de 2011? Da dos ideas.

Any TWO of:
Una investigación (por el estado)
Descubrieron mucha corrupción
Representantes acusados (de corrupción/abuso de poder) [2]

Finally, the recording revisits the fatal crashes mentioned in question **(b)**. This question asks you to provide two direct results of the crashes. The fact that 40 people died is relevant to question **(b),** but to answer this question you should stick with the information that is provided in this section of the recording:

*Después de los choques en 2011, el Estado instigó **una investigación** sobre el ministro de transporte que reveló **una extendida red de corrupción**. Como resultado, **muchos representantes fueron acusados** de corrupción y abuso de poder.*

Any TWO of these events would gain you full marks: firstly, that the state initiated an investigation into the ministry of transport, and secondly that this investigation revealed widespread corruption. As a result of this, many representatives were accused of corruption and abuse of power. Try to make your answers as concise as possible; it is not necessary – or indeed possible – to quote every single thing that you hear in the recording.

Mark Scheme:

0/2	- Information is not supplied or not relevant.
1/2	- Candidate has identified and supplied one correct direct result of the fatal crashes in 2011.
2/2	- Candidate has identified and supplied the two correct and separate direct results of the fatal crashes in 2011.

Full transcript

M: *Una nueva serie de trenes de alta velocidad en China se lanzará este mes. Una mayor velocidad significará que el viaje desde Shanghái a Beijing durará tres horas y media, una hora y media menos que actualmente. En 2011, la velocidad de estos trenes fue limitada por el Gobierno, después de dos choques que mataron a cuarenta personas. Los nuevos trenes viajarán a una velocidad media de 350 kilómetros por hora y los ingenieros creen que podrían ser aun más rápidos con mejoras en las vías, hasta 400 km/h.*

Tendrán un sistema de control que reducirá la velocidad automáticamente en caso de emergencia. Además de esto, habrá un aumento de confort para los pasajeros, con más espacio para las piernas, comida caliente y acceso gratis a Internet. Después de los choques en 2011, el Estado instigó una investigación sobre el ministro de transporte que reveló una extendida red de corrupción. Como resultado, muchos representantes fueron acusados de corrupción y abuso de poder.

END OF SOLUTIONS FOR PAPER 4

Oral (speaking) Primer

Visit **www.rsleducational.co.uk/spanishaudio** to download the conversation recordings discussed in this guide.

The recordings demonstrate how to approach the oral examinations in Spanish and feature a genuine GCSE student. They cover the **conversation** section of the oral exam. This is the part that many students fear most, and may not know how to prepare for properly.

This section of the pack explains how to improve your grade in this part of the exam, and also provides mark grids.

According to the exam board you are with, other sections of the oral exam may include a role play, a short presentation (with follow-up questions from the examiner), and/or a pre-prepared description of a picture of your choice (with follow-up questions). Some boards use a mixture of these.

Exams involving role-play and/or presentation sections are best prepared for by revising the conversation topics below, making sure you have learnt topic-specific vocabulary and expressions. You can also use the **example questions on pages 146-8** for this purpose. You can then practise saying in class what you've learnt here. Your teacher will be able to guide you further, according to your exam board.

Mark Scheme

There are three mark grids to be applied to the general conversation section: communication and content, interaction and spontaneity, and linguistic knowledge and accuracy. These are worth 12 marks each, giving a total of **36 marks**.

The following mark schemes are **designed to cover all exam boards** and can be used by all students.

The breakdown of the **Communication and Content** section looks like this:

Communication and Content

0	- No rewardable material
1-3	- Candidate communicates some relevant information according to the topic and question, occasionally extending their sentences. - Candidate gives straightforward ideas and opinions, occasionally justifying them. - Candidate's vocabulary is limited and straightforward, sometimes resulting in limited communication. - Candidate's pronunciation is often intelligible and clear, with occasional inaccuracies resulting in lost clarity of communication.
4-6	- Candidate communicates relevant information according to the topic and question, with some extended sequences of speech. - Candidate occasionally uses creative language to express opinions and ideas, and occasionally justifies them. - Candidate's vocabulary features some variety, including some uncommon or complex language, resulting in mostly clear communication. - Candidate's pronunciation is intelligible, with minimal inaccuracies that do not result in lost clarity of communication.
7-9	- Candidate communicates relevant information in detail according to the topic and question, usually extending their sentences and sequences of speech. - Candidate frequently uses creative language to express and justify ideas and opinions. - Candidate's vocabulary varies, including frequent uncommon language and a variety of expressions. - Candidate's pronunciation is often intelligible and predominantly accurate.
10-12	- Candidate communicates detailed and relevant information according to the topic and question, consistently using extended sequences of speech. - Candidate uses creative language to express and justify a wide variety of ideas and opinions throughout. - Candidate uses a wide variety of vocabulary, including frequent uncommon language, and a variety of expressions/structures for different purposes. - Candidate's pronunciation is consistently intelligible and accurate.

In other words, you are required to use language **creatively** to convey your ideas and experiences. Use as much topic-specific vocabulary as you can, as well as interesting expressions. For help with this, see my *Steps to a Higher Grade* document (**page 149**), and use it to come up with ideas of your own too.

Mistakes are not the end of the world, and perfection is not expected at GCSE level, so be **bold** with your answers and try not to just give the bare minimum response. Instead, look to **extend** your sentences with conjunctions such as *porque, sin embargo, además de* etc. You can also **link** various ideas with *también, por una parte/por otra parte, aunque* etc. in order to get your point across in an **interesting and convincing** way. Finally, practice makes perfect! Practise with friends, teachers and others to gain confidence, as well as practising your Spanish accent so that everything you say can be understood.

Next, let's see the breakdown for the **Interaction and Spontaneity** section:

Interaction and spontaneity

0	- No rewardable material
1-3	- Candidate only occasionally responds spontaneously, and is often stilted, but with some examples of natural interaction. - Candidate occasionally initiates conversation and independently develops ideas, but requires frequent prompting. - Candidate occasionally sustains communication, with frequent hesitation.
4-6	- Candidate responds spontaneously to some questions, with natural interaction for parts of the conversation. - Candidate initiates and independently develops the conversation sometimes, with some prompting needed. - Candidate sometimes sustains communication, sometimes with rephrasing, self-correction or repairing phrases, and with some hesitation.
7-9	- Candidate responds spontaneously to most questions, with natural interaction for most parts of the conversation. - Candidate mostly initiates and independently develops the conversation. - Candidate sustains communication throughout most of the conversation, sometimes with rephrasing, self-correction or repairing phrases if needed, and with occasional hesitation. **[P.T.O.]**

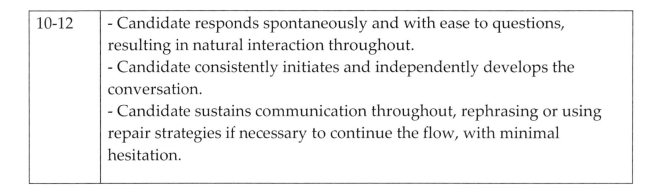

10-12	- Candidate responds spontaneously and with ease to questions, resulting in natural interaction throughout. - Candidate consistently initiates and independently develops the conversation. - Candidate sustains communication throughout, rephrasing or using repair strategies if necessary to continue the flow, with minimal hesitation.

Again, your answers don't have to be perfect: the exam is intended to mimic a real-life conversation and has to sound **natural**. Therefore, a bit of hesitation and pausing is to be expected. Likewise, don't rush through your answers at break-neck speed, as this sounds unnatural. Do, however, respond promptly to the question.

You are also expected to **help** the conversation along, and develop it. So **add in your own ideas** and **lead the discussion** towards issues that you know how to talk about. In this way, you can guide your examiner to questions you have practised. Don't just give the bare minimum response!

If you do make a mistake, or need a bit more time to understand the question, you can ask your examiner with **repair phrases**, such as those below. Make sure to keep speaking in Spanish though – **never** revert to English or another language! This way, you can still convey your answer, even when you are struggling. For example:

¿Me puedes repetir la pregunta por favor? = Please can you repeat the question?
¿Puedes decir la pregunta de nuevo más despacio/de otra manera? = Can you say the question again more slowly/in another way?
¿Qué quieres decir con eso? = What do you mean by that?
¿Qué dijiste…? = What did you say?
Bueno, vamos a ver… = Well, let's see…
¡Vaya pregunta tan difícil/interesante! = What a difficult/interesting question!
Nunca me he fijado en eso antes, pero… = I have never thought about that before, but…
(Lo que) quiero decir… = What I mean to say is…
Digo… = I mean (when self-correcting)
Lo dije por error/me equivoqué. = I said that by mistake.

Try not to rely on these phrases, but you can use them if you are struggling and need a bit of help or time to think.

Finally, the breakdown for **Linguistic Knowledge and Accuracy**:

Linguistic Knowledge and Accuracy

0	- No rewardable material
1-3	- Candidate manipulates a limited variety of mainly straightforward grammatical structures, with minimal use of complex structures. - Candidate uses some accurate grammatical structures, and some successful past, present and future tense conjugations, although with some ambiguity. - Candidate sustains sequences of coherent speech, although errors often hinder clarity of communication and meaning.
4-6	- Candidate occasionally demonstrates a variety of grammatical structures, with some use of complex structures, although with frequent repetition. - Candidate uses generally accurate grammatical structures, and generally successful past, present and future tense conjugations. - Candidate sustains generally coherent speech, although with errors that sometimes hinder clarity of communication and meaning.
7-9	- Candidate manipulates a variety of grammatical structures, with some variety of complex structures. - Candidate uses predominately accurate grammatical structures, and mostly successful past, present and future tense conjugations. - Candidate sustains predominately coherent speech, with errors rarely hindering clarity of communication and meaning.
10-12	- Candidate manipulates a wide variety of grammatical structures, with frequent use of complex structures. - Candidate uses consistently accurate grammatical structures, and consistently successful past, present and future tense conjugations. - Candidate sustains fully coherent speech, with errors not hindering clarity of communication and meaning.

Therefore, try and use complex structures in your responses. Use the *Steps to a Higher Grade* document to help with this: fill it in with some of your own ideas too. You are expected to attempt to use longer sentences, with a range of parts of speech, such as pronouns, conjunctions, adverbs and adjectives, and **avoid repetition** where possible. Also, you must try and provide a range of tenses when prompted: if the question is about your future plans, you must answer with the future tense; if it is about your past experiences, you must answer in the past!

Even this section of the mark scheme, which focuses on accuracy of language, does

<u>not require error-free Spanish</u>! Nevertheless, any errors must not get in the way of your meaning. You can come back and self-correct if you like, or rephrase what you are trying to say. Incorrect gender or adjectival agreements aren't major, mark-losing errors. However, using the incorrect **person** or **tense** with a verb can often be confusing to the examiner and will be penalised. Also, make sure you answer the question you are asked – talking about something unrelated will be construed as a mistake!

To sum up:

The **golden rules** for the oral exam are very similar to the model approach to the long writing question at the end of each reading/writing paper in **Volume 2**:

- ✓ Use **past, present, and future** tenses, including with irregular verbs.
- ✓ **Justify** your opinions.
- ✓ **Don't be boring**! Use interesting vocabulary and a wide variety of structures, with minimal repetition.

The Recordings

Now, listen to the recordings of a real GCSE student (see **www.rsleducational.co.uk/spanishaudio**). They cover **three** conversation topics, though in your exam you will probably only have time for two – or perhaps even one, if your answers are detailed enough! The marks I have given each recording are quite severe for the sake of highlighting the strengths and weaknesses of different approaches.

Recording – Topic Area A: Home and Abroad

In this conversation, the student does very well in using interesting vocabulary to answer each question, consistently changing the linguistic structures that she uses. She shows a lot of **ambition**, particularly in the more challenging questions, using difficult structures such as the subjunctive: *si tuviera…* She always **expands** her answers, giving examples linking sentences. There are a few grammatical and pronunciation mistakes but, on the whole, these do not make her answer incomprehensible to a native speaker, and so these are considered minor errors. There is some hesitation in her answers, but again, this is minimal and she always responds to the question accurately and promptly. Where there is hesitation within a response, she usually corrects herself or finds another way to say it.

Communication/Content	10
Spontaneity/Interaction	11
Linguistic Knowledge/Accuracy	12
Total (Out of 36)	33

Recording – Topic Area B: Education and Employment

In this recording, the student was asked to take a slightly different approach, and continue to expand her answers until she ran out of things to say. Sometimes the examiner will interrupt to ask a related question, but it is a good strategy to be able to keep **expanding** on your sentences where possible. Here, the student is able to offer new information, often by giving examples or counter-arguments. There is some hesitation and stumbling over words, which has perhaps come from trying to get too much information out quickly, but the standard of her responses is consistently very high, using different tenses, and the subjunctive where relevant. Again, there are some pronunciation issues and the odd gender disagreement, but not enough to severely hinder communication.

Communication/Content	12
Spontaneity/Interaction	11
Linguistic Knowledge/Accuracy	11
Total (Out of 36)	34

Recording – Topic Area D: The Modern World and the Environment

In this recording, the student and the examiner keep the conversation flowing, so it is more natural. Nonetheless, the student still expands her answers where she can. The pronunciation is generally intelligible, although with a few errors, and there is the odd grammatical mistake too. However, she is given a lot of credit for attempting some more advanced grammatical structures. This is a slightly more challenging topic than the previous ones, and the range and level of vocabulary the student uses to respond to the questions is consistently good.

Communication/Content	10
Spontaneity/Interaction	11
Linguistic Knowledge/Accuracy	11
Total (Out of 36)	32

Example questions

The following list is not exhaustive, but it demonstrates the standard range of questions that will be asked by your teacher/examiner. They are designed to test your vocabulary and your ability to express and justify your opinions, as well as your ability to use the present, past, and future tenses when appropriate. Use them to practise!

Topic Area A – Home and Abroad

➤ Describe dónde vives.

➤ ¿Qué tiempo hace?

➤ ¿Qué se puede ver y hacer en tu ciudad?

➤ ¿Qué piensas de tu ciudad/región?

➤ ¿Dónde te gusta pasar las vacaciones?

➤ Describe tus últimas vacaciones.

➤ ¿Cuáles son tus planes para las próximas vacaciones?

➤ ¿Cuál sería tu destino ideal para ir de vacaciones? ¿Por qué?

➤ ¿Por qué es importante viajar al extranjero?

➤ ¿Cuáles son las ventajas y desventajas de vivir en una ciudad/en el campo?

➤ ¿Prefieres ir de vacaciones con tu familia o con tus amigos? ¿Por qué?

Topic Area B – Education and Employment

- ➤ Describe tu instituto.
- ➤ Describe tu rutina escolar.
- ➤ ¿Cómo vas al instituto?
- ➤ ¿Qué asignaturas te gustan/no te gustan?
- ➤ ¿Qué te pones para ir al instituto?
- ➤ ¿Qué te gusta/no te gusta de tu instituto? ¿Por qué?
- ➤ ¿Estás a favor o en contra del uniforme escolar? ¿Por qué?
- ➤ ¿Qué opinas de las reglas/normas de tu instituto?
- ➤ ¿Los deberes son importantes?
- ➤ ¿Qué hiciste ayer en tu instituto?
- ➤ ¿Qué planes tienes para el próximo año/el futuro?
- ➤ ¿Cuál sería tu trabajo ideal?
- ➤ Describe tu experiencia laboral.
- ➤ ¿Es importante la experiencia laboral?

Topic Area C – House, Home and Daily Routine

- ➤ Describe a tu familia.
- ➤ Describe dónde vives.
- ➤ ¿Dónde te gustaría vivir en el futuro?
- ➤ ¿Qué haces con tus amigos?
- ➤ ¿Qué haces para ayudar en casa?
- ➤ ¿Qué hiciste el fin de semana pasado?
- ➤ ¿Qué sueles comer y beber durante la semana?
- ➤ Describe la última vez que fuiste a un restaurante.
- ➤ ¿Cómo te llevas con los otros miembros de tu familia?
- ➤ ¿Quiénes son más importantes para ti – tu familia o tus amigos?
- ➤ ¿Tu familia lleva una dieta sana?

Topic Area D – The Modern World and the Environment

➢ ¿Qué haces en casa para ayudar al medio ambiente?

➢ ¿Qué haces para ayudar al medio ambiente en tu instituto?

➢ ¿Por qué es importante el medio ambiente?

➢ ¿Utilizas las redes sociales?

➢ Describe tu programa de TV, o película, o libro favorito.

➢ ¿Tienes móvil? ¿Cuándo lo usas?

➢ ¿Qué haces en el ordenador en tu casa / en el instituto?

➢ ¿Prefieres ver las películas en la televisión o en el cine?

➢ ¿Cuáles son las ventajas/desventajas de los móviles/Internet?

➢ ¿Qué importancia tiene Internet en tu vida?

Topic Area E – Social Activities, fitness and health

➢ Describe tu último cumpleaños.

➢ ¿Qué haces en tu tiempo libre?

➢ ¿Qué tipo de música te gusta?

➢ ¿Qué haces normalmente los fines de semana/ por las tardes?

➢ ¿Vas de compras con frecuencia? ¿Dónde? ¿Qué compras?

➢ ¿Qué haces para mantenerte en forma?

➢ Describe un fin de semana ideal. ¿Qué harías?

➢ ¿Te gusta el deporte?

➢ ¿Te gusta la música?

➢ ¿Llevas una vida sana?

➢ ¿Qué piensas del tabaco / del alcohol / de las drogas?

Steps to a Higher Grade

How to boost your written and oral responses

Below are some surefire ways of upgrading the quality of your work in all papers. Some of these tips are simply words or phrases you can use; some are more general ideas and suggestions as to how to approach the exams. You don't have to use all of these things in an answer, but it's a good idea to sprinkle them liberally throughout your work.

If I were to condense my advice down to **four essential steps**, they would be:

1) Past tenses*
2) Future tenses*
3) **Justified** opinions
4) Don't be boring!

* Examiners will expect you to conjugate verbs in the present tense without difficulty.

Without following the four essential steps above, it is **impossible** to gain full marks on any of the papers.

Let's look at these four points in more detail:

Essential Step 1 – PAST TENSES

There are a number of ways to talk about things in the past in Spanish. Here are some of them.

a) <u>Preterite tense</u>

Try to use at least **three** examples of the Preterite tense (including an **irregular)** in any extended piece of writing or speaking.

Use the Preterite tense:

✓ **To tell of something that happened** *once.*

Fui ayer a la tienda = I went to the store yesterday
Escribí la carta = I wrote the letter

✓ **To tell of something that happened** *more than once but with a specific end.*

Fui ayer a la tienda seis veces = I went to the store six times yesterday
Leyó el libro cinco veces = He read the book five times

✓ **To indicate** *the beginning or end of a process.*

Hace tres años aprendí tocar el piano. = Three years ago, I learned to play the piano.
El huracán se terminó a las ocho. = The hurricane was over at 8 o'clock.

b) Imperfect tense

Try to use at least **one** example of the Imperfect tense.

Use the Imperfect tense:

✓ **To tell of past** *habitual or repeated actions.*

Cuando era joven, escribía muchas cartas. = When I was young, I used to write many letters. (NOTE: Sometimes in English, 'would' is used instead of 'used to' to express the imperfect tense: *When I was young, I <u>would</u> write many letters.* Don't get this confused with the conditional tense!)

✓ **To describe a** *condition, mental state or state of being* **from the past.**

Había una casa aquí. = There used to be a house here.
Quería ser feliz. = He wanted to be happy.
Tenía frío. = He was cold.

✓ **To describe an action that occurred** *over an unspecified time.*

Se lavaban los manos. = They were washing their hands.
Mientras José tocaba el piano, María comía. = While José was playing the piano, María was eating.

✓ **To indicate** *time or age* **in the past.**

Era la una de la tarde. = It was 1 pm.
Tenía 43 años. = She was 43 years old.

TOP TIP: Telling the difference (Imperfect vs. Preterite)

To sum up, the Preterite tense is for finite (limited/completed) events, where the end of the process has been seen, whereas the Imperfect tense is ongoing or unspecified. Use the Imperfect tense for **descriptions** and **ongoing/incomplete actions** in the past (*I was doing* etc.), and the Preterite tense for **finished actions** in the past. (*I did* etc.)

I was doing something when something else **happened** - the "doing something" is the background action (imperfect) and the "happened" is the completed action (preterite): *Hacía* algo cuando otra cosa **pasó**.

---

c) Perfect tense (present perfect)

Use the Perfect tense for a **recently** completed action, i.e. something that *has* happened.

Ya he comido. = I have already eaten.
Ella ha ido a España con su novio. = She has gone to Spain with her boyfriend.

d) Pluperfect tense (past perfect)

Use the Pluperfect tense for a completed action **far in the past**, i.e. something that *had* happened.

Ya había comido. = I had already eaten.
Ella había ido a España con su novio = She had gone to Spain with her boyfriend.

The Pluperfect tense is often used together with the Preterite to describe **two past events, one of which occurred before the other**:

Ya había comido cuando volvió mi madre. = I had already eaten (pluperfect) when my mother returned (preterite).

Try and use at least **one** perfect (*has done*) or pluperfect (*had done*) tense in your responses.

Essential Step 2 – FUTURE TENSES

There are a number of ways to talk about things in the future tense in Spanish. Try to use at least **three** examples, including **irregulars**.

a) Informal future

You can also use the Informal Future to talk about what IS GOING TO happen (we have a similar construction in English), using *ir + a + infinitive*.

Voy a ir al colegio mañana. = I am going to go to school tomorrow.
No me va a escuchar. = He is not going to listen to me.

b) Simple future

Use the Simple Future to talk about what WILL happen. This is harder than the Informal Future, but for that reason, will gain you extra marks.

Iré al colegio mañana. = I will go to school tomorrow.
No me escuchará. = He will not listen to me.

c) Conditional tense

Try to use at least **one** example of the Conditional tense, to talk about what you or someone else WOULD like or do:

> *Me gustaría ir a España.* = I would like to go to Spain.

… or what WOULD be the case or happen (hypothetically):

> *Él sería un buen actor.* = He would be a good actor.

Essential Step 3 – JUSTIFIED OPINIONS

It's not enough to say whether you like something (or not): you have to say **why** (or why not)! Try to use at least **three** justified opinions, in a variety of ways - don't be boring!

a) Express your opinions.

Use a variety of the following examples to introduce your point of view…

> *(No) Pienso que…/creo que…/opino que…* = I (don't) think that…

> *En mi opinión/Según yo/Desde mi punto de vista…* = In my opinion/According to me/From my point of view…

(No) me gusta/encanta/flipa/apasiona/chifla(n) etc. = I (don't) like/love/am passionate about/am crazy about.

b) Justify them!

…And don't forget to <u>explain why</u> you feel that way! Don't just use *porque*. Here are some examples of other ways of justifying your opinions:

ya que = since
dado que = given that
puesto que = since/given that

Essential Step 4 – DON'T BE BORING!

The final step is to keep your answers as interesting as possible. Here are some tips:

a) Interesting adjectives

Inolvidable = unforgettable
Imprescindible = essential
Vergonzoso = disgraceful

When you come across more adjectives that you find interesting, write them down here! Continue on a separate sheet if necessary.

b) <u>Interesting adverbs</u>: ~~*Muy*~~ —> *extremadamente/verdaderamente*

Instead of a "boring" adverb like *muy* (very), trying more interesting intensifiers, such as those above (extremely/truly). If you think of or come across any more, write them down here!

c) <u>Avoid repetition.</u>

Think of synonyms and more interesting ways to express yourself without repeating yourself.

Instead of this …

Me gusta jugar al fútbol porque es muy divertido. También me gusta la música, sobre todo la música rock porque es muy divertida.

(= I like to play football because it's very fun. I also like music, especially rock music, because it's more fun than classical music.)

… why not try this:

Me encanta jugar al fútbol porque es extremadamente divertido. También me apasionan todos los tipos de música, pero el género que más me gusta es la música rock ya que la encuentro mucho más emocionante que la música clásica.

(= I love playing football because it's extremely fun. Also, I am passionate about all types of music, but the genre I like best is rock music because I find it a lot more exciting than classical music.)

Notice how the second version is immediately more interesting (which will impress the examiner, and also make it easier to remember than a boring sentence!)

d) <u>Reduce the number of simple verbs.</u>

For example, instead of this …

Comí ese burrito porque me gusta mucho la comida mexicana.

= I ate that burrito, because I really like Mexican food

… why not try this:

Devoré ese burrito porque me flipa la comida mexicana.

= I devoured that burrito, because I am mad about Mexican food

e) Connecting words

Make sentences longer by connecting them:

e.g.   *que* = that, which, who
        mientras = whereas, while
        porque = because
        puesto que = given that (see #3b))
        cuando = when

You can **expand on** or **explain** your previous sentence:

e.g.   *o sea* = in other words
        es decir = that is to say
        por ejemplo = for example
        tal(es) como = such as
        así que = so
        por lo tanto = therefore

f) Use a variety of structures and vocabulary.

Boost the quality of your written and spoken Spanish and keep it interesting! Here are some examples of constructions that examiners typically look for.

✓ *Tener* **phrases**

Spanish uses the verb *tener* a little differently than we use the verb 'to have'. For example, rather than <u>being</u> hungry or hot, you say you <u>have</u> hunger or heat. This kind of construction often expresses a physical **sensation**:

tener calor = to be hot

tener frío = to be cold

tener hambre = to be hungry

tener sed = to be thirsty

tener sueño = to be sleepy

Or psychological **feelings**:

tener celos = to be jealous

tener confianza = to be confident

tener cuidado = to be careful

tener miedo a/de = to be afraid of

tener prisa = to be in a hurry

Or one of the following:

tener la culpa = to be guilty

tener éxito = to be successful

tener ganas de = to feel like/want

tener lugar = to take place

tener que = to have to

tener razón = to be right

tener suerte = to be lucky

✓ **Decidir** + INFINITIVE = to decide (to do something)

You don't need *que* or *a* after *decidir*, just the <u>infinitive</u> (the unconjugated form) of the verb.

Decidí salir anoche. = I decided to go out last night.

✓ **Sin** + INFINITIVE = without

Sin perder un momento = Without wasting a moment

✓ **Antes de/después de** + INFINITIVE = before/after

Antes de llegar… = Before arriving…

Después de comer, me fui. = After eating, I left.

✓ **Al** + INFINITIVE = <u>On</u> (doing something)

Al llegar, me sentí muy cansado. = On arriving, I felt very tired.

✓ *Para* + INFINITIVE = In order to (do something)

Para ver a mi amigo, tengo que coger el tren. = In order to see my friend, I have to take the train.

✓ **Exclamations**

¡Qué rollo! = What a bore!

¡Qué asco! = How disgusting!

¡Qué buena idea! = What a good idea!

✓ *A pesar de (que)* = despite (the fact that)

Use an **infinitive** after *de* and a **conjugated** verb after *de que*

A pesar de no tener dinero, lo compré. = Despite having no money, I bought it.

A pesar de que no tengo dinero, lo compré. = Despite the fact I have no money, I bought it.

✓ *Acabar de* + INFINITIVE = To have just…

Examiners love testing this verb, because you only have to use *acabar de* in the present to express *having just done* something, and you don't have to use the perfect tense. Remember to include *de* because *acabar* on its own means to finish.

Acaban de construir unas casas nuevas. = They have just built some new houses.
BUT: *Acaban mis exámenes en junio.* = I finish my exams in June.

✓ *Estar a punto de* + INFINITIVE = To be about to…

Using this in the present allows you to introduce talking about **future** actions, without actually using a future tense.

Estoy a punto de hacer mis deberes. = I am about to do my homework.

Estaba a punto de salir cuando sonó el teléfono = I was about to go out when the phone rang.

✓ **Comparatives**

Compare by saying something is <u>more</u> … than (<u>*más*</u> … *que*) or <u>less</u> … than (<u>*menos*</u> … *que*).

Es más guapo que yo. = He is more handsome than me.

Estoy menos gordo/a que mi madre. = I am less fat than my mother.

Mejor/peor que… = Better/worse than…

If something is <u>as</u> big/fast/intelligent etc. <u>as</u> something else (i.e. the <u>same</u> as), use *tan … como*:

Es tan rápido como Usain Bolt. = He is as fast as Usain Bolt.

No es tan guapa como mi novia. = She is not as pretty as my girlfriend.

✓ **Superlatives**

Whereas a comparative is bigger/better/smaller/worse etc. than something, a superlative is the big<u>gest</u>/best/worst etc.

Using *lo* with a superlative means <u>the</u> biggest/best/worst etc. <u>thing</u>.

Ella es la más rica = She is the richest (person)

Lo más importante es… = The most important thing is…

Lo mejor/Lo peor = The best thing/The worst thing

✓ **Negatives**

Spanish uses **double negative** constructions to create negative expressions: using nothing/nobody/nowhere etc. plus *no*. In English this would sound a bit odd ('I didn't say nothing'), but it is correct in Spanish: *no dije nada*.

Nada = Nothing

No *hay* **nada** *allí.* = There's nothing there.

Nunca/jamás = Never

No *iré* **nunca** *a Francia.* = I will never go to France.

Nadie = Nobody

*No había **nadie** en casa.* = There was nobody at home.

Ninguna parte = Nowhere

> *No lo encuentro por **ninguna parte.*** = I can't find it/him anywhere.

Ni … ni = Neither … nor

> *No quiero ir al cine **ni** al restaurante **ni** al museo.* = I don't want to go to the cinema nor to the restaurant nor to the museum.

Tampoco = (N)either

> *Yo **no** voy, y tú **tampoco**.* = I'm not going, and neither are you.

✓ **Desde hace** = since

Use *desde hace* with **present tense** (not perfect) tense and a plural noun.

> ***Vivo** en Londres desde hace cinco años.* = I have been living in London for five years.

NOT: **He vivido en Londres desde hace cinco años*

> ***Estudiamos** español desde hace tres meses.* = We have been learning Spanish for three months.

NOT: **Hemos estudiado español desde hace tres meses*

✓ **Pronouns**

For example: *Me gusta **ella*** = I like her

> *Me acompañó **mi** madre* = My mother came with me

✓ **Subjunctives**

Finally, subjunctives are used to express things that are hypothetical, or to express opinions and doubts. This is technically an A-Level structure, but it's worth learning a range of subjunctive phrases and using at least **one** in your work, because it will get you extra marks:

*Me gusta que **sea** divertido/inteligente/rápido etc.* = I like that it/he is fun/ intelligent/fast etc.

*Cuando **sea** mayor.* = When I am/he/she/it is older.

*Me **hubiera gustado** quedarme más tiempo.* = I would have liked to stay longer.

*Ojalá **pudiera**.* = If only I could.

*Ojalá **fuera** posible.* = If only it were possible.

Quisiera … = I would like…

NOTE: *Quisiera* is the Imperfect subjunctive of *querer*, but is commonly used to mean "I would like" instead of the Conditional tense of *querer*. This is mainly because *querría* (I would like/want, Conditional tense) is virtually indistinguishable in spoken Spanish from *quería* (I wanted, Imperfect tense).

BV - #0010 - 160320 - C6 - 297/210/9 - PB - 9780993467462